How God Became African

How God Became African

African Spirituality
and Western Secular Thought

Gerrie ter Haar

PENN

University of Pennsylvania Press
Philadelphia

Published by
University of Pennsylvania Press
Philadelphia, Pennsylvania 19104-4112

Printed in the United States of America on acid-free paper
10   9   8   7   6   5   4   3   2   1

Library of Congress Cataloging-in-Publication Data

Haar, Gerrie ter
  How God became African : African spirituality and western secular thought / Gerrie ter Haar.
      p.   cm.
  Includes bibliographical references and index
    ISBN 978-0-8122-4173-0 (alk. paper)
    1. Christianity—Africa.   2. Spirits.   3. Supernatural.   4. Africa—
Religion.   I. Title.
  BR1360.H23   2009
  235.096—dc22   `2009017226

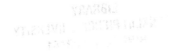

Contents

Preface

How God Became African explores the ways in which the Christian God has in Africa assumed features that are deeply rooted in the continent's own religious history. The continuing importance of religion in Africa, including Christian religion, cannot be understood without reference to this longer history.

Accordingly, the first chapter provides an explanatory framework for the book, introducing some of the key issues and the threads that connect the following chapters. The first part of the book, Chapters 2–4, provide an insight into the various ways Africans have incorporated Christianity and adapted it to the realities of their own culture and history. In particular, the first part of the book discusses Africans' belief in, and experience of, a spirit world. Together, these chapters introduce the reader to particular aspects of African Christianity that are usually unfamiliar to non-Africans. With this background the second part of the book takes us away from the immediate sphere of the spirit world and more toward the human world, considering how African religious ideas have affected society and continue to do so.

Christianity has a long history in North Africa, going back to the time when it was part of the Roman empire. This region produced some of the greatest leaders of the early Church, including such famous names as Clement, Origen, Tertullian, Cyprian, and Augustine of Hippo, all of whom made the Church a thriving force in antiquity. The Ethiopian Church and the Coptic Church also have historical credentials dating from this early period.

It was generally not until the fifteenth century that any endeavor was made by Europeans to launch Christian missionary activity in Africa. This was first attempted as part of a wider expansion of exploration and trade at that time, notably from Portugal. It led in particular to the conversion of an African king, the ruler of Kongo, a kingdom situated in what is now northern Angola and western Democratic Republic of Congo. The Christian kingdom of Kongo was recognized by the pope, but it did not survive beyond a few generations. In subsequent centuries, this early missionary impulse was followed by others, but none of this early activity had an impact on the same scale as the nineteenth-century European missionary enterprise, when Christian religion rooted itself definitely in Africa.

From its early beginnings until today, African Christianity has consistently shown an openness to the kind of spirit-oriented experiences that have characterized many of the nineteenth-century revival movements in Europe and North America. The belief in and the practicing of spiritual gifts, known as *charismata*, is common among Christians in Africa. The word "charisma" is used in the Bible to describe a wide range of metaphysical experiences. It is derived from the Greek word for grace, χάρισμα, and refers to the grace of God through the Holy Spirit. There is thus a high degree of historical continuity between present-day neo-pentecostal and charismatic churches and ministries in sub-Saharan Africa and the early nineteenth-century churches that implanted themselves in the region during the religious revival movements of that century.

The revivalists became known for their use of spiritual gifts, such as prophecy, healing and speaking in tongues, all of which were seen as manifestations of the Holy Spirit, as described in the New Testament. The nineteenth-century religious revivals led to intensified missionary activity on the part of Protestant churches in many parts of Europe, following the foundation of various mission societies in the late eighteenth and early nineteenth centuries.

Little would those early missionaries have imagined that two centuries later the roles would be reversed, with African missionaries coming to reconvert Europe. Africa is no longer only on the receiving end of the missionary relationship but has become a sending continent, even though it continues to receive far more foreign missionaries than it sends out. In an age of international migration, African Christians are establishing congregations worldwide, with the result that African missionaries can be found in every continent. African Christians often consider Europe a spiritual desert, ripe for evangelization, in a surprising reverse of the nineteenth-century missionary tradition.

In the present book I have focused on how the Christian God has changed. We must be aware, however, that there are other religious traditions in Africa that have also undergone significant changes in the course of time. This concerns notably Islam, which took root in Africa long before Christianity did. But the same is true of other religions. Africa houses an enormous diversity of religious tendencies, from traditional and neotraditional movements to imported religions such as Christianity and Islam in all their rich diversity. Less well known is that Eastern religious movements are also present in many countries in Africa, some of long standing and others rather newer, of Hindu and Buddhist extraction. And we should not forget the various mystical movements of European origin, such as Freemasonry and Rosicrucianism, as well as New Age movements originating in the United States. These examples are intended only to give an impression of the vitality and dynamics of the religious landscape in Africa, a useful perspective since African societies have often been represented as fundamentally static and unchanging. Those who are familiar with Africa will know it as a religiously vibrant continent that absorbs new trends rather easily by adapting them to its own needs.

The obvious dynamism of religion in Africa has caused many Western observers in recent years to suggest that Africa is currently undergoing a religious revival. This statement seems to be not quite accurate, as religion has never been absent. We may put the matter otherwise by suggesting that observers who identify a religious revival in Africa today are in many cases simply noticing for the first time the importance of the religious dimension in African societies; in previous decades, the secularization of Western societies caused many academics and others to suppose that Africa's development would inevitably consign religious belief to a minor place. Most recently, worldwide interactions between politics and religion since the start of the twenty-first century have made religion a subject of the greatest political salience. This has contributed to a growing awareness of the continuing significance of religion in most parts of the world.

Chapter One
God in Africa: Some Key Issues

Religion, Spirituality, and Science

It can hardly escape anyone traveling to Africa that religious belief and practice are a normal part of the social fabric in most communities. Yet, there are some important differences from the ways in which Europeans and North Americans, raised in societies with different historical and cultural backgrounds, generally understand "religion."

In Africa, "religion" refers to a widespread belief in an invisible world, inhabited by spiritual forces or entities that are deemed to have effective powers over the material world. This definition of religion emerged from the specific context of Africa, where the perceived spirit world has a considerable and real presence. In that sense it is quite different from definitions derived from modern Western experiences, which tend to consider religion in terms of a search for ultimate meaning in life.[1] The African understanding comes much closer to the meaning of the Latin original *religio*, a word that first appeared in the third century B.C.E. in reference to Roman religion, of which divination was a central feature. Cicero, in particular, glossed *religio* as the conscientiously performed worship that is due to the gods. The worship to which Cicero referred was a response to the continuous stream of revelatory messages that the Roman gods were believed to send to the world of humans, the content of which could become known through divination. Under the influence of the Church a shift eventually took place from this classical Roman view to a specifically Christian articulation of religion, and the older Roman religion became categorized as "superstition," the negative counterpart of the "real" religion of Christianity.[2] This pattern of classification has been continued ever since by European intellectuals in regard to many non-Western forms of belief and practice. Thus it was in conformity with a longstanding practice that early European missionaries in Africa, as well as colonial officials, came to consider indigenous African religions as belonging to a residual category that included—to use the vocabulary of the nineteenth century—polytheists, animists, and idolaters.[3]

This short exposition does little justice to the complex semantic history of the term "religion." It does, however, serve to draw attention to the variety of ways terms and concepts are used and understood in actual practice. A continual problem in writing about religion with regard to Africa is the words we use, which are often value-laden. The terms in which the religious traditions of Africa are often described by social scientists continue to show signs of the colonial heritage, reflecting the unequal relationship of that era. The choice of terminology is not a neutral matter, as history shows, and in many cases African religious beliefs continue to be seen in terms that have a derogatory connotation and emphasize the difference between "us" and "them." Hence, while "we" are religious, "they" are superstitious, and while our beliefs may be "mystical" in nature, theirs belong to the "occult," just to mention some conceptual categories and terms that have been indelibly marked by the historical processes of Africa's evangelization and colonization. It is important to be aware of this legacy in order to equip ourselves with terms and concepts that are morally neutral and that may be applied to religious phenomena worldwide, and not only in regard to Africa. An uncritical use of conventional categories hampers our understanding of significant aspects of the religious life of many Africans today, including the large numbers of Africans who now live in Europe. Modern connotations of "religion" are the result of a long theistic tradition, conditioned by the history of Europe rather than by Africa's own history.

The power to choose and use a particular terminology with which to describe the realities of other people has long been a Western privilege, and continues to be so. An openmindedness toward unfamiliar phenomena, such as some of those discussed in the present book, is further hampered by the secular orientation of many Western societies, in which substantial numbers of people consider religion an outdated mode of expression. It is also useful to maintain an open mind concerning the way power relations between different peoples manifest themselves in language. Hence it becomes crucial to ask the question: who defines what and for which purpose? This is a question I will return to in this book when discussing issues related to African identity. The identification by European thinkers and administrators of certain practices as being either religious or superstitious in nature has had a formative effect not only on Africa but also on societies in many other parts of the world. The way indigenous practices in relation to an invisible world have been construed by writers, politicians, and officials as either "religion" or "superstition," or they have been labeled by some other name, is a process that has had a great bearing on perceptions of spiritual power and on the moral value attached to attempts to access such power. As will become clear from the discussions in this book, this process has also had a considerable impact on the way African Christians are viewed in the West.

Such matters are eminently cultural. I am aware that the concept of culture has become discredited in recent years, notably in anthropological circles, for a variety of reasons. However, my own years of research have left me with the conviction that African "culture" matters to Africans. I mean by this not that there exists a single, authentic African culture, but that many Africans believe that there are ways of being in the world that are characteristic of people from Africa. Whether this is an intellectually sound position depends greatly on one's definition of "culture." Of all the definitions in existence, the one that strikes me as most appropriate for present purposes is that by the nineteenth-century anthropologist E. B. Tylor, who defined culture simply as all that a human being learns or acquires as a member of society.[4] This is a definition in which human society—and nothing else—is the criterion of culture. Defined in that sense, "culture" is not only about human behavior, but also about ideas. Both behavior and ideas change over time. Culture and cultures are historically contingent.

African culture matters to Africans as a question of identity and self-esteem. Perhaps even more important, African culture matters to them because they believe it has a contribution to make to global culture. This fact is frequently overlooked by non-Africans, who for reasons of their own often prefer to see Africa as a continent sui generis instead of as part of the world. This book considers Africa a normal part of the world, and thus as a meeting place of different cultural influences, of which Christianity is a major one. It is in this context that the concept of inculturation becomes important, referring to the process by which Christian evangelization assumes the characteristics of various cultures. Processes of inculturation and contextualization have drawn the so-called world religions and ethnic religions closer to each other, in the sense that their relationship to, and embedding in, a specific culture form a common element between them. African Christianity, both in its behavioral expressions and in its patterns of thought, is thus culturally shaped, but not fundamentally different in its various manifestations. This is notwithstanding some views to the contrary, which will also be discussed in this book.

Inculturation is an issue discussed in more detail in Chapter 2, as a necessary step in the exploration of more specific aspects of African Christian identity that will take place in subsequent chapters. Crucial here, I will argue, is the way African believers consider the spirit world. African Christians bring with them their own spiritual ideas, in a process of inculturation. Europe in particular has been slow to accept the implications of this historical development. To corroborate my argument, I have taken as an example the life of Emmanuel Milingo, former Roman Catholic archbishop of Lusaka, the capital city of Zambia, who was removed from his episcopal see as a result of his controversial healing ministry.[5] His African-informed understanding of the spiritual needs of his parishioners led him on a track that took him from Lusaka to Rome and eventually to the United States. He now lives in Washington as a married man, associated with the church of Reverend Sun Myung Moon, popularly known as the Moonies, a church of Korean origin. The question is what went wrong in a career that took off so brilliantly and ended in a dispute that could have split the Catholic Church? The answer, I suggest, lies in the issue of inculturation, both a problem and a challenge for the universal Church.

Emmanuel Milingo, born in 1930, was ordained in 1958. He was appointed archbishop of Lusaka in 1969, at a time that the Catholic Church, in the wake of African nationalism and political independence, was beginning to give preference to African leadership. A man of outstanding abilities, Milingo was deemed able to steer the Zambian Church into a new future. Widely known already for his pastoral concern, he became closely involved in the personal problems of his congregation. In 1973 he reached a turning point in his life when he was confronted with the despair of a woman who believed herself to be possessed by evil spirits and felt a compulsion to kill her newborn baby, of which she had developed a morbid fear. Medical and psychiatric cures having failed, she had turned to the archbishop for help. In a dramatic encounter that he himself has described in one of his numerous writings, they both felt overpowered by the Holy Spirit during a prayer session, as a result of which the woman was liberated from the evil spirits that she believed to have power over her. She became totally healed and no longer feared her baby. From that moment, Milingo began to realize that his long years of priestly training had not prepared him to deal with the spiritual needs of his own people. He subsequently set out to develop a healing ministry within the Church, for which he based himself on the authority of the Bible. Yet, this became a bone of contention leading to a conflict with the Catholic Church that has never been resolved.

Milingo's views on healing are closely related to his understanding of the spirit world. In fact, his spiritual beliefs provide the key to understanding his healing ministry, in which liberation became a central issue. Healing, in his view, is a comprehensive concept that does not limit itself to a physical cure, but is concerned with all aspects of suffering, including those affecting people's moral and spiritual life, thus addressing the whole person. Similarly, when healing occurs, he believes, it does not limit itself to the individual but also affects the life of the community and of society at large. Healing, then, means taking away any disturbance in life that prevents a person from being fully human; or, in other words, to help someone overcome a stumbling block on the road to human fulfillment. It implies restoring original wholeness and returning him to his original dignity. To do this, one has to remove every form of oppression and disturbance in life, irrespective of its cause. Spiritual healing, in his experience, is fundamental to the development of a healthy society. In Milingo's thought, liberation became an idea that he further developed and related to ideas of emancipation and identity concerning Africans and the African continent, as well as their spiritual and material development.

Archbishop Milingo is not alone in his views about the need for a comprehensive healing ministry in Africa. Religious healing, as we may call this type of healing, is central to most religious traditions in Africa, and the Western-rational neglect of this need, in and outside church circles, appears time and again to create problems in the relationship between Europe and Africa, and even, in a wider sense, between the Western and non-Western world. It is an important reason for the proliferation of independent churches in Africa, where religious healing is commonly practiced, meeting a basic need of many people in Africa. Today, many people are attracted to the new charismatic churches precisely because of their active healing ministry, which explicitly addresses the powers believed to reside in the spirit world. Their spiritual basis has two pillars, deriving from a deeply rooted indigenous African religious tradition on the one hand, and the Christian religious tradition on the other.

Most African religions are traditionally charismatic in character: they make allowances for active communication with a spirit world and even allow for people to become possessed by the perceived inhabitants of that world. This forms the subject of the third chapter of the book. Africans generally believe that direct communication with the invisible world is possible. They are far from alone in this belief, as there are many societies that have developed techniques for communicating with a perceived spirit world. In many cases, communication with the invisible world that people believe to exist is based on systematic thought and experimentation. "Spiritual technology," as we may call the elaboration of such methods, aims at awakening and mobilizing human faculties in reference to a spiritual world that is considered to be a source of real and effective power. Believers may use spiritual technology in an attempt to improve their material life. This is a subject that I return to in Chapter 6.

A common way of interacting with the spirit world in Africa is by means of spirit possession. Neurobiological research suggests that this is a universal human potential that is mediated through culture. Christianity in Africa, too, has increasingly adopted a charismatic character, making space for the presence of the Holy Spirit, which, when it comes, is believed to come with power, manifest in the person who is overpowered by the Spirit. While in the West people generally shy away from such behavior, in Africa it is not particularly remarkable, as it relates to cultural patterns of behavior with which most people are familiar. In fact, possession trance behavior is quite common throughout the world. This is confirmed by several studies done in the 1970s when there was a significant interest in altered states of consciousness, at a time that in western Europe and the United States a youth culture was flourishing that was widely associated with the use of consciousness-expanding drugs. According to one study, of a sample of 488 societies in all parts of the world, 437, or 90 percent, had some institutionalized, culturally patterned form of altered states of consciousness, and 251, or 52 percent, interpreted the trance experience in religious terms.[6] These findings suggest that it is not Africa, or any other non-Western society for that matter, that is exceptional in this regard, but rather Western society that forms an exception when it comes to trance behavior.

Like all patterns of human action, possession behavior in Africa is to a large extent learned behavior, acquired by individuals over time in contexts where it is submitted to social and ritual control. It usually takes place in public. Spirit possession is therefore quite different from a mental or psychiatric disorder, as outsiders who are unfamiliar with the phenomenon of possession often claim it to be. Seen in this light, exorcism can be considered to constitute a form of ritual control over demonic possession, which can lead to effective healing.[7] However, the fact that spirit possession implies a form of learned behavior, influenced by cultural expectation, does not mean that it can occur in certain societies only, and not in others. For the neurobiological structures that make possession behavior possible are shared by all human beings. Scientific research on the connection between neurobiology and spirit possession is controversial, as it requires the interpretation of data that are at the very limits of scientific knowledge. Above all, research on this matter extends into the field of religion, which causes many scientists almost instinctively to be on their guard. They may suspect that nonscientific methods and arguments are being deployed and that the whole subject comes uncomfortably close to a metaphysical realm that is not a proper object of inquiry for scientists.

However, recent research using classic scientific methods does suggest some new and interesting ways of understanding spiritual phenomena for which there otherwise appears to be no rational explanation. It is for this reason that they are often relegated to the realm of fantasy, or ascribed to false consciousness or mental illness or other such categories that lack explanatory power. The majority of natural scientists adhere to an exclusively materialist paradigm of the world. But there are some who are open to wider explanations for phenomena of a spiritual nature and who are prepared to go beyond a materialist paradigm. Researchers of this type take a more holistic approach in their efforts to explore new avenues of inquiry. What these scholars seem to share, in the words of one of the best-known writers in this field, biochemist and cell biologist Rupert Sheldrake, is an objection to "the closed-minded dogmatism" that makes many scientists afraid to go beyond convention.[8] Sheldrake has become known for introducing the idea of so-called morphic fields and the related concept of morphic resonance. He applies these ideas to memory, among other things. Drawing on the work of French philosopher Henri Bergson, he proposes that memory is inherent to all organically formed structures and systems, especially organisms. He argues that bodily forms and instincts, while expressed through genes, do not have their primary origin in them. Instead, his hypothesis states, the organism develops under the influence of previous similar organisms through morphic resonance.[9] Another eminent scholar venturing outside the conventional borders of his discipline is British scientist Roger Penrose, who has written extensively on the connection between fundamental physics and human consciousness. In his book *The Emperor's New Mind*,[10] he argues that the known laws of physics are inadequate to explain the phenomenon of human consciousness. In the field of philosophy there are also reputable scholars who have been similarly bold in going beyond standard fields of explanation. One such scholar is David Chalmers, professor of philosophy and director of the Centre for Consciousness at the Australian National University, who is known for his scholarly work on the human mind. Chalmers also argues that conventional explanations of consciousness in terms of physical processes are inadequate.[11] Neuroscience, in his view, will be a (major) part of a new and more comprehensive theory that will bridge the gap between science and subjective experience.

The point of these examples is not to suggest that these scholars are necessarily correct in their views—in any case, I am not competent to judge in the matter—but to draw attention to the fact that there are internationally reputed scholars whose views may be controversial and not widely accepted by their peers, but who nevertheless enjoy sufficient prestige within their discipline that their views cannot be dismissed out of hand. The reason I am referring to them at the present juncture is because their theories open a potential avenue for understanding the type of experiences that many Africans claim in relation to a believed spirit world.

The following paragraphs reflect some of these ideas, which may suggest a degree of explanation for the type of spiritual experiences discussed in the first chapters of this book. I base myself in particular on a study by Dutch cardiologist Pim van Lommel, who has conducted scientific research into near-death experiences.[12] Published in book form in 2007, Van Lommel's findings followed an earlier article by himself and others in *The Lancet*, a leading journal in the field of medical research.[13] This article drew worldwide attention at the time of publication. In my view, Van Lommel's book is highly relevant to the subject of the present discussion regarding Africans' experiences of the spirit world. The main findings are summarized below.

During his career Van Lommel has regularly been confronted with patients who have survived a cardiac arrest. Some of these patients were able to describe their experience during the period when their heart had stopped. They consistently related how, while being aware of their physical death, they underwent an experience of existing outside their physical body. In this state, they experienced an exceptional clarity of consciousness, accompanied by a perception of existing in a dimension without time and distance. They were able to envision both past and future. During this period they felt themselves to be in a condition of utter peace. Trained in the conventional materialist tradition of science, Van Lommel was struck by the consistency of these narratives. Rather than dismissing such stories on the grounds that they were not explicable within the dominant scientific paradigms, and could therefore not be "true," he resolved to undertake a systematic study, as the frequency with which experiences of this type were reported suggested the need for a more thoughtful answer. In particular, the descriptions given by his patients raised some unexplainable questions about the relationship between human consciousness and the brain. He therefore undertook a long-term prospective study into near-death experiences, based on controllable observation.

Normally speaking, once all the brain functions have ceased to work, a patient is pronounced clinically dead. In this condition, it should be impossible for a person to experience any form of consciousness at all, since scientists generally believe the brain to be the source of human consciousness. Hence, the most common explanation for near-death experience is a lack of oxygen feeding into the brain. Nevertheless, there are neuroscientists who have proposed that a purely materialist explanation of consciousness is untenable. Instead, they suggest, the brain is not the producer but rather the facilitator of consciousness. Comparing the human brain with modern communication media may be helpful at this point. According to the hypothesis, the brain may be compared to a computer that is connected to the Internet. The computer does not produce the information that appears on the screen, but only facilitates its reception. The data do not originate inside the apparatus. Reception can be deactivated by switching off the machine, but the information continues to flow. Similarly, the brain may be compared to a television set that captures broadcast images that it does not itself produce. In both cases there is a continuous flow of information around the globe in which time and distance seem no longer to apply. This is similar to the theories of consciousness and the brain referred to above: like the Internet and television, the brain, too, does not produce human consciousness. It only makes it possible for human beings to experience a consciousness that is nonlocal.

On the basis of his research, Van Lommel has come to the conclusion that conventional scientific theories about near-death experience are unable to present a comprehensive theoretical explanation for this phenomenon, leaving many questions unanswered. He proposes a theory of nonlocal consciousness that is based on concepts derived from quantum physics, a branch of scientific theory that dramatically challenged Newtonian physics during the twentieth century. Van Lommel suggests that nonlocal consciousness may exist in the form of so-called probability waves, a concept used in quantum physics to denote an individual electron that may exist either as a particle, when it is measured or located, or as a wave, in which case it has no specific location. According to this analogy, nonlocal consciousness provides the brain with information but also receives information from the body and the senses via the brain. The brain is thus a transceiver, comparable to a television set, which receives information from electromagnetic fields that it decodes into picture and sound, and also to a video camera that turns picture and sound into electromagnetic waves.

In such a view, human consciousness is not confined to the brain, since consciousness is nonlocal and thus lacks a material basis, and since the brain has a facilitating function that enables a person to experience consciousness. The brain does not have a consciousness-producing function, according to this view; it rather makes the experience of consciousness possible. Modern brain research also suggests that human consciousness has a direct influence on the function and anatomy of the brain, probably connected to the role of DNA. Consequently, there are researchers who specialize in investigating the possible connection between modern science and the great contemplative traditions, especially Buddhism. Over centuries, these religious traditions have investigated the nature of consciousness using their own methods and techniques, such as meditation. There appears to be growing evidence that meditation can effect a change in the brain as a result of the brain's plasticity, a characteristic that distinguishes the brain from the hardware of a computer or a television. In short, modern brain research suggests that science may be feeling its way toward an epistemological shift concerning the nature of reality and human consciousness. It may provide explanations for meta-physical experiences that conventional scientific theories are currently unable to explain. This includes not only near-death experiences but also other experiences of a spirit world, such as are widespread in Africa.

Although it would be premature to conclude that quantum physics can provide an explanation for meta-physical experiences, Van Lommel and some other scientists believe that its foundational concepts indicate a plausible direction toward an explanation for phenomena that cannot be explained with reference to concepts and categories derived from classical physics. The concept of nonlocality implies forms of connectedness that are independent of time and distance. For present purposes, the most interesting form of connectedness is that between the material and the perceived spirit world of Africa. Nonlocality also hints at an explanation for the type of spiritual experiences that are discussed in Chapter 4, some of which clearly resemble a near-death experience. The idea of a nonlocal and literally endless consciousness may incorporate a range of other religious experiences commonly encountered in Africa, including visions of the type reported by African prophets, and an enhanced intuitive sensitivity such as that apparent in African healers. By reference to concepts now widely accepted in physics, mystical experiences may become more intelligible, including the experience of enlightenment or mystical union. In the vocabulary of quantum physics, such personal experiences of the absolute ground of life may be explained by analogy with the quantum vacuum, sometimes described as "a field of infinite potentiality."[14] Similarly, what Africans consider communication with a spirit world may become intelligible in quantum terms as a form of interaction with a nonlocal consciousness; the latter, as explained above, may be considered as the source of human consciousness. In such a view nonlocal space is a meta-physical space, which can nevertheless be influenced by human consciousness, since the human brain has a quality of adaptation known as neuroplasticity that distinguishes the brain from a machine.

Religious experiences of the sort discussed here, spiritual or mystical experiences, then, cannot convincingly be explained simply as products of the brain. Such experiences may be better understood as facilitated by the brain in ways that require further scientific research.

Whether or not scientific research makes progress in this direction, the fact is that Africans, like people in other societies with long religious traditions, have established techniques and standard means of communication with an invisible world. The latter is usually represented as a world of spirits that is a source of power. Therefore, the spiritual experiences referred to at length throughout this book are considered by many Africans to be direct infusions of power. Spiritual power becomes *real* power for those who believe in it, having an effect on individuals and communities. People who believe themselves, and are believed by others, to be in direct communication with a spirit world are considered to be powerful. This includes a whole range of religious specialists from a variety of persuasions or traditions, and many such people are perceived as having a religious vocation, usually revealed to them through a specific spiritual experience or event.

This mode of thinking about a spirit world has also been assimilated by African Christians, and African Christians find a basis for this in the Bible. A person called by the Spirit—whether the Holy Spirit or any other spirit—is charged with a responsibility for the community that is often born out of pain. Religious vocations tend to follow a standard pattern, beginning with illness and eventually ending in a form of miraculous salvation that convinces others. While entirely credible in an African context, miracles tend to pose problems to the Church as an institution, since it has itself grown very skeptical of their occurrence in modern times. Miracles have a long history in European Christianity and have subsequently been exported to other parts of the world as the Christian religion has spread. The most famous ones in the Western world have been recorded within the Catholic belief system. They are often connected with the appearance of the Virgin Mary, but may also take different forms, notably through healing or stigmata, the bodily marks of the crucified Christ. Their fame is due to recognition by the Catholic Church as a "true" miracle, which then allows for a cult to be established at the place of occurrence. In such a case the miracle has been "canonized" and thus put under the control of the Church. In other words, it has become domesticated.

This is particularly the case in regard to miracles said to have occurred in

Africa, where miracles cannot easily be kept under control. Since Christianity has been implanted on the African continent, Christian miracles have become very common. The Virgin Mary, for example, no longer appears exclusively to white Europeans in places such as Lourdes, Fatima, or Medjugorje, but also shows herself freely to black Africans, where she may assume a black skin.[15] This example shows an interesting contextualization of Christian miracles. It also demonstrates the potentially subversive character of belief in spiritual power when it encounters other forms of power. Thus, in a continent where the realms of religion and politics have an impact on one another, miracles may also acquire political significance. Religion and politics in Africa constitute two important realms of life, distinct but not separate, providing rival sources of power that may be pursued simultaneously. Ensuring access to spiritual power is a preoccupation of many people in Africa, both at the bottom and at the top of society. Miraculous events are one remarkable way to win support for political claims, taking the study of miracles beyond the field of religion.

In the last decade of the twentieth century miraculous events have been reported from all parts of the world, including different continents and different religions. They include Muslim and Hindu examples. An Islamic miracle, for example, was reported from Mombasa, where, in 1992, a "holy message" mysteriously appeared on a wall, containing the Muslim creed in Arabic script. In the mid-1990s, the international press reported extensively on a Hindu miracle implicating a statue of the god Ganesha, the well-known deity with the elephant head, which—to the amazement of many people— had been seen drinking milk. Miraculous events have also been ascribed to the Cuban "anti-communist saint" Elian, the young boat refugee who in early 2000 was at the center of a political dispute between Cuba and the United States. Apparitions of the Virgin Mary have frequently been reported, and in 1996 crowds of people flocked to Clearwater in Florida to put flowers and candles in front of a building that on Thanksgiving Day miraculously showed a picture of Mary on one of its glass walls. In contemporary Europe, too, there appears to be a clear increase in the belief in miracles. In the Netherlands, for example, in 1991 32 percent of the population showed a positive interest in miracles; ten years later this applied to 47 percent of the population. This trend is still growing, providing statistical evidence of a postmodern worldview that has opened itself up to spiritual experiences that seem to defy a long tradition of Western rationality. Reports about weeping statues of the Virgin Mary abound, and Web sites have been created on her apparitions that are classified according to the grade of official approval they have received. In

1997 a weeping statue of Elvis Presley in the south of the Netherlands became world news. Spiritual healing and trance experiences are fairly common in Europe today, while pilgrimage has become a popular form of tourism, and apocalyptic belief causes hardly any embarrassment. In its wondrous beliefs, Europe is perhaps less different from Africa than would appear at first sight.

Religion, Society, and Global Awareness

A need for inculturation expresses itself not only in the field of religion, but equally in the sphere of specifically contemporary concerns, such as human rights (more fully discussed in Chapter 5). The modern concept of human rights has been formed in response to profound experiences of evil, notably the horrors perpetrated by the Nazis in the death camps during the Second World War. For an effective implementation of human rights worldwide, a cultural understanding of evil seems crucial, though it is often neglected by human rights activists. This is remarkable, given that reference is often made in the West to a human rights "culture." It suggests a way of life that is defined by a particular understanding of what human rights are, assuming that this is shared globally. In fact, it appears that people's understanding of what human rights are is influenced by their own cultural understandings and experiences, including in Africa.

Africans, it seems, generally consider that human rights—whether or not they are known by this name—cannot be detached from a religious understanding of evil. That is, human rights have to be seen in relation to people's belief in a spirit world. The persistence of belief in the presence of evil, and the concomitant belief in the need to combat it, is in fact one of the contentious issues in relations between former mission churches in Africa and homegrown African-initiated churches, in and outside the African continent. At the same time, this is an issue that connects the earliest African independent churches and the latest generation of charismatic churches in Africa, in spite of their individual differences. The common thread is a consciousness of the presence of evil, and the need to counter it, in whatever form it may appear.

This can be seen notably in regard to witchcraft beliefs, which are both strong and widespread in Africa, and often result in witchcraft accusations that lead to serious human rights violations. Many Africans consider witchcraft a spiritual form of evil that humans may manipulate intentionally and unscrupulously to further their own interests. European missionaries, and colonial officials as well, often supposed that, since at some stage in history witchcraft persecutions had ceased in Europe, they were likely to stop at a certain stage in Africa too; this is an argument that can still be heard today. Witchcraft belief and witch-hunting in Europe—so the argument goes—were the products of ignorance and eventually terminated due to human progress in the form of a more enlightened approach to religion, the advance of science, and the correct use of reason. African reality shows how superficial such comparisons are, based on an evolutionary approach to the passage of time that lacks historical contextualization. It also shows how spiritual realities in Africa continue, at least by implication, to be seen in terms of superstition. It is significant, in this respect, that there are many educated Africans who are well versed in Western culture and science but may nevertheless believe in the existence of witchcraft powers. This goes to show how deeply concepts of evil are culturally embedded. Africans' cultural understandings of evil, then, must also be considered in the light of the global movement for human rights.

Concepts of evil are central to the religious beliefs of many Africans. They have been so in the past and continue to be so in present times. Yet, their relation to human rights is usually not considered, either by human rights lawyers or by others with a professional interest in human rights. International human rights discourse has tended to develop an exclusively moral-legal approach, due to its singleminded emphasis on only one dimension of the concept of human rights. It has failed to pay due attention to the first element of the composite term—the human dimension—which in many parts of the world suggests the usefulness of a moral-spiritual approach. The exclusively legal approach of most human rights discourse poses problems for religious believers worldwide, who tend to attach great importance to the spiritual dimension of a person in the belief that this is what makes someone truly human. Hence, there is a general need, in my view, to look closely at the role of religion in regard to human rights, since an exclusive rights approach that fails to take into account the question of what actually constitutes a human being will not yield the desired result of protecting human rights worldwide. Secular human rights activists easily disagree with those who do not base their concept of rights in the first instance on a human source, but locate its origins in some divine or supernatural or spiritual power. Instead of becoming allies in the fight for human rights, they often end up as ideological enemies with seemingly different interests. For a successful human rights policy, it appears, the two dimensions must be in balance. This can only be achieved if secularists are prepared to make use of existing spiritual resources, and if religious people are prepared to appreciate and ally themselves with secular approaches.

Underlying the above discussion is a fundamental question: how can religion, or the religious resources present in a given society, be used for the protection and promotion of human rights and thus for the prevention of human rights violations? Religious resources are, after all, human resources. This is an important question, first of all because so many people practice religion, but particularly because of the universal aspiration of the idea of human rights.

Human rights and development are generally considered to be closely related. This is manifested in the so-called rights-based approach to development that has been adopted in recent years by most development organizations, both governmental and nongovernmental, in donor countries as well as by international organizations. Yet, it is not altogether clear what precisely this may mean. Some critics have even suggested that "rights-based" has become the latest item in development fashion, used to dress up the same old-style development practice.[16] Others have argued that today's rights-based development discourse needs to be critically interrogated in order to see where it is coming from. Who is articulating it? What are the differences in the versions used by various development agents, and what are their shortcomings? What implications do these have for the practice and politics of development, compared to other approaches?[17]

A religious or spiritual approach to development is one such form of critical interrogation. A critical engagement of religious approaches to development with secular ones is not intended to replace the latter, but to complement them (as explained in Chapter 6). This is a line of thought that is increasingly followed by policy-makers in the West who have begun to realize the shortcomings of an exclusively secular approach to the challenge posed by development. Our earlier exposition on religion as a form of active engagement with a world of invisible powers is relevant in this regard, since it has a bearing on people's views of the material world and the ways they deal with it. Seen in this way, religious ideas and the practices derived from them are of obvious relevance to development agents. Not only should development policy-makers be aware of this fact, but, more important, they should explore ways of using people's religious or spiritual resources for the sake of development. Spiritual empowerment, or empowering people through spiritual means, has the potential to become a serious option in development cooperation, alongside material forms of empowerment.

There has for years already been a reaction against approaches to development that place technical aspects and goals ahead of the needs of individuals. Newer approaches have sought to place people at the centre of development, and the concept of human development has now gained widespread currency. Thus, when the first Human Development Report was launched in 1990, it was "with the single goal of putting people back at the center of the development process in terms of economic debate, policy and advocacy." As the report made clear, this was expected to have far-ranging implications, going beyond monetary income to assess the level of people's long-term well-being. Development of the people, by the people, and for the people was stated to be the ultimate aim, emphasizing that the goals of development are choices and freedoms.[18]

From this perspective, spirituality, or religion more generally, becomes an aspect of human development. Yet the potential of religion and spirituality for development is seldom considered, and little thought has been given to how religious resources can be used for development. This omission is remarkable in view of the fact that the majority of people in the world adhere to some form of religious belief that guides their daily actions. Effective development requires a mobilization of a full range of human resources. It should start from people's own worldviews, which in many cases are religious. In Africa, too, development must take as its starting point Africans' specific understanding of the world, which in most cases includes the realm of the invisible.

Historically speaking, people in all parts of the world have assimilated and adapted notions of development that were originally conceived in Europe and exported largely through the colonial process. Various societies have brought, and still bring, their own ideas to notions of development and progress. These ideas are often articulated in a religious idiom, not least because the notions of development and religion have so much in common. They both contain a vision of an ideal world and the place of humans therein. It is not difficult to find examples of the ways people's religious understanding of the world may have a bearing on development. The traditional Hindu idea of humankind, for example, emphasizes harmony with the living environment. This easily translates into a view that economic growth should be integral to the well-being of the environment as a whole. Similarly, Muslims believe that the ultimate aim of life is to return humanity to its creator in its original state of purity. In African traditional religions, the pursuit of balance and harmony in relations with the spirit world is paramount. Charismatic Christians (of whom there are large numbers in Africa and in developing countries more generally) believe that personal transformation—inner change—is the key to the transformation of society. All these ideas inevitably shape people's views of development.

In contemporary Europe, politics and states have taken over the ideas of perfection that had previously been related to the spiritual sphere. In the twentieth century this led to a great variety of political projects aspiring to create a model society that some have described as "coercive utopias," secular ideologies that aspire to create a model society.[19] With hindsight we may consider that "development" was one of the many coercive utopias of the twentieth century, which inherited some of the ideology and techniques of religion. The idea of development may be seen as the secular translation of an originally religious belief concerning the attainment of a perfect world.

A related idea is the belief in progress, which is also a fundamental Christian notion reflected in much modern development thought. The idea that humankind is bound to progress on the way to a materially better world is central to the project of development. As far back as 1976, Archbishop Milingo of Zambia, referred to above, made a similar point when he gave a series of lectures concerning the subject "Awareness of the World Around Them" to students of the Divine Word Centre in London, Ontario.[20] He noted on that occasion that the English dictionary suggests the word "progress" as a synonym for development. "Progress," in his view, is about purely material advancement. It stands for "external human achievement in a community of men," or, in other words, "the advancement into stages of anything that can externally be observed."[21] "Development," by contrast, refers to a process that leads to a change of attitude and helps people become self-reliant. "Living with human problems, they must know how to solve these problems and hence uplift themselves from the mire of misery, degradation and distressing situations. That is why heaping material goods into the hands of the 'have-nots,' without taking into consideration their own involvement in overcoming poverty, has brought no development to the people concerned."[22] It is quite ironic that such an analysis was made more than thirty years ago by an African prelate who has gained his reputation in the Western world as an exotic and otherworldly priest. These days, many Western development agents would readily agree with Milingo that human development cannot be equated with the material progress of a nation. Holistic development, as it is often referred to, is increasingly considered to be characteristic of human development in the broad sense.

Religion continues to be important to people, even when they move to other continents, and religious belief continues to guide their daily actions. International migration is without doubt one of the most significant features of contemporary globalization; African migration is a significant component of it. In the present book this is discussed with particular reference to Europe, since African migration is a relative novelty there compared to the United States.[23] Today, African migrants can be found everywhere, from North America to Europe, from Japan to the Middle East, and from the former Soviet republics to Australia. Many of them have traveled in search of work, with a view to improving the material conditions of their families and communities in their countries of origin. Given the size of the remittances they send home, migration and development have become two sides of the same coin. Here, too, the spiritual aspect plays an important role, as African economic migrants, many of whom lack legal status, use their religious belief to improve their own condition. In an age of international migration, African Christians are establishing congregations worldwide. This includes Europe, where African immigrants have given a new impulse to the spiritual condition of the continent through the foundation of new churches, as discussed in the last chapter of this book.

African immigrants in Europe use the spiritual power at their disposal to sustain their material existence, as they often live in materially poor conditions, particularly if they stay in the host country illegally. Their religious communities help to create the holistic circumstances of individual well-being that may enable members to contribute to the development process in their country of origin. From a believer's perspective spiritual empowerment, therefore, is an effective strategy, since it opens up alternative avenues to achieve what is often referred to as the "good life." The point in this respect is that it is the same spiritual power that equips African migrants with the basic condition for contributing to the development process. The economic development of the home country cannot be detached from the personal development of African migrants.

The social significance of religion can hardly be understood without reference to its actual content. For African Christians in the Netherlands, for example, the substance of their religion is contained in the Bible. The importance they attribute to the Bible is common to evangelical Christians the world over, but must also be understood in the light of the specific experiences of African Christians who have migrated to Europe. They use the Bible to build themselves spiritually and to criticize in a spirit idiom what they see as unjust social structures. By reading the Bible, they believe, they will get to know the will of God and receive clear directions concerning both society at large and their individual selves. This does not mean that the Bible is held to provide readymade answers to every question; rather, it is thought to contain the key to the answer to any question. Identifying the key means opening the way to the right path, allowing the individual to take a first step in the proper direction. It is just another example of the way the material and the spiritual worlds of Africa are interconnected, or, from a Christian perspective, the human and the divine. The indivisibility of the visible and invisible worlds remains central in the Christian thought and practice of Africans, whether they live in Africa or outside.

Religious Ideas as Key to Understanding Africa

Spiritual knowledge is for most Africans a valid and legitimate type of knowledge. Although they distinguish between the material and the spiritual spheres of life, they do not separate the two in the same way as is characteristic of intellectual traditions in the West. African traditions of thought tend to view reality not in terms of binary oppositions and mutually exclusive categories—in other words, in terms of either/or. Rather, they tend to view reality in categories that are inclusive—in terms of and/and. Hence, in African discourses, a person can be considered as being dead while physically alive, like a zombie, a living person who is spiritually dead. Vice versa, a person can be physically dead, but considered to be spiritually alive, like an ancestor. Thus, people may be invisible, yet "really" present, in the form of spirits, which so many Africans believe to exist. The same logic applies in African Christianity, in which the invisible world is perceived to have a real existence and to interact with humans in the visible, material world.

By the same token, spirit and reason are not mutually exclusive categories in African traditions of thought. In this regard, it is notable that recent research in both the natural sciences and academic philosophy seems to be opening new avenues for exploring the relationship between the physical world and the human mind. This suggests the possibility that certain modes of apprehending reality that are common to African worldviews and often represented in religious terms may also find explanations couched in the language of science. This should not, however, be taken to imply that African believers will cease to accept the reality of a spirit world. This is precisely, as suggested above, because they do not consider spirit and reason incompatible and exclusive categories.

The ideas referred to in previous lines are fundamentally religious in nature, if we define religion contextually, as I do throughout this book. Religious ideas, in this sense, suffuse African thinking generally. They are also key to such pressing global concerns as human rights and development in Africa. For this reason, it is important to take Africans' religious ideas into account even in dealing with matters that, internationally, are often seen as fundamentally secular concerns.

The need to take African epistemologies more seriously, even when these are of a religious nature, imposes itself all the more urgently in the light of large-scale international migration. Many Africans in recent years have moved to other continents, taking their religious ideas with them. African modes of thought have been spreading as a consequence, especially through the activities of African Christians, who have set up new churches worldwide. Africans have assimilated Christianity, both spiritually and socially. This first happened in Africa, but it is now also occurring outside. Clearly, the story of how the Christian God became African is continuing.

Chapter Two

How God Became African: A Continuing Story

Perhaps the greatest surprise of the twenty-first century is the resilience of religion. This is true of Africa as of many other parts of the world that were formerly colonized by Europe.

Rather than declining in importance, as theories of secularization and modernization had predicted, religious belief and practice appear to have been on the increase in Africa, to the extent that both academics and journalists have been suggesting that a religious revival has taken hold of the continent. I would like to suggest that such an assessment is not correct, since religion has always been a vibrant element of African societies. In fact, it tells us more about the observers than about the object of their observations, since so many of them have a secular outlook that has blinded them to Africa's continuing religious dynamics. If this situation has changed relatively recently, it is largely due to a growing perception that religion has implications for politics and state security. Nevertheless, there is undoubtedly a revitalization taking place in regard to Africa's religious traditions, which has led to a renewed assertiveness that is manifested in the public domain. This is mostly evident in regard to Christianity and Islam. Both of these religions were originally imported into Africa, but Africa has now become fully integrated into their global histories. Although Christianity is a relatively new religion in most of Africa, the speed with which the Christian God has adopted an African character, in spite of substantial Western reticence, is quite spectacular.

If we leave aside the early history of Christianity in Africa, significant as it may be (consider Egypt, Ethiopia, North Africa), it is astonishing how in a historically short period— basically since the nineteenth-century missionary enterprise—the Christian religion has taken root in Africa.[1] The most spectacular growth of African Christianity occurred in the last quarter of the twentieth century, in the wake of Africa's political independence. Available statistics suggest a growth from fewer than 9 million African Christians in 1900 to some 350 to 400 million in 2000, almost one in five of all Christians.[2]

The 2008 statistics indicate even more rapid growth since the start of the twenty-first century, to a projection of almost 630 million in 2025.[3] These statistics should be considered in the wider context of the growth of Christianity in the non-Western world, with the most recent figures clearly demonstrating the numerical prominence of Africa, Asia, and Latin America.[4] If Africa's growth trend were to continue, it would soon become the continent with the largest number of Christians, a position currently still held by Europe.[5] As Ghanaian theologian Kwame Bediako has consistently argued, Christianity has today become a "non-Western" religion, with more Christians in the southern than in the northern hemisphere.[6] What we do not yet know is whether and how this will affect the life of the Church worldwide, at both the theoretical or ideological and the practical level. In the present book I explore some aspects of African religious thought and practice to imagine ways the Christian God may continue to become ever more African.

Compare this evolution to the prospect at the beginning of the nineteenth century. A Victorian missionary would probably have been surprised by the success story of Christianity in sub-Saharan Africa. Never would he or she have expected Africa to become the leading continent in steering the course of world Christianity. As a thought-experiment, compare this to the way Chinese might replace English as the dominant language in business and education if China becomes the world's largest economy. Ask yourself what difference it would make if indeed Africa were to become the leading continent for Christian thought and practice.

The difference, I suggest, might be as significant as that between the English and the Chinese languages, as the cultural roots of African Christianity are far removed from its cradle in the West, the place from where the continent was evangelized. Most of all, it would affect the role of the Holy Spirit—in Western Christianity typically the poor relation of the Holy Trinity—which would grow to prominence at the expense of God the Father, who might be pushed off his ecclesiastical throne. African spirituality, I suggest throughout this book, is crucial to understanding Christianity as it has taken shape in Africa itself and outside Africa through migration. In view of the fact that by the year 2050 a substantial part of western Europe may be "black" as a result of international migration,[7] Europe may well develop a Black Church tradition rooted in African soil, as has happened in the United States as a result of forced migration at the time of the slave trade.

African Traditional Religions and Christianity

The spirit-oriented nature of African Christianity builds on the indigenous religious traditions of Africa, which postulate the existence of a spirit world, with many inhabitants with whom direct communication is possible. This is particularly notable in the African independent churches, commonly referred to in the academic literature as AICs. AICs are indigenous churches that came into existence originally in the late nineteenth century in response to the mission activities of the historical mainline churches in Africa. They have emerged on the initiative of African people outside the direct context of the missions, and are led by Africans. Hence they are better described as African-initiated churches, an appellation that emphasizes the African initiative in global Christianity.[8] They are characterized by unique forms of social and political organization, and have developed their own doctrines on the basis of Christian belief.[9] Although they are generally categorized into one large group, there is great diversity among them, and scholars have generally found it difficult to propose a clear typology.[10]

A number of factors account for the emergence of these home-grown churches,[11] including disappointment with aspects of Christianity that were ill adapted to the African context; translation of the Bible into local languages, which led to various forms of reinterpretation and spiritual renewal among African Christians; and inadequacy of the mainline churches in the face of the needs of African believers. These shortcomings were felt most notably in the important field of healing and medicine. This continues to be the case. Spiritual healing is an outstanding characteristic of African independent churches, as it is of most new religious movements in Africa. It is a form of religious healing whose prevailing mode of expression is one in which the spirit world holds a central place. In addition, one of the main strengths of African independent churches is their capacity for community building. In general, it can be said that at times of drastic social change these churches have proved able to build new moral communities, and have shown themselves capable of fulfilling an important role both in the new urbanized context of Africa and in the rapidly changing rural areas. But such is equally true of the independently founded African churches outside the continent, including in Europe (discussed in more detail in Chapter 7).

In 1984, generally considered the AIC centenary year, it was estimated that there were about 12,000 independent churches on the African continent, with a total membership of 30 million.[12] Since then their number has increased, particularly since the emergence of the latest growth in African

Christian independency, most notably in the form of charismatic churches. These are African-initiated churches that, unlike their predecessors, are characterized by a distinctive global outlook and orientation. Furthermore, as indicated above, African independent churches of different types have recently also emerged outside the continent as a result of international migration, including in Europe. This latest trend in particular has brought a new dynamic to relations between churches in Africa and Europe.

In the course of history, African Christians have contextualized Christian missionary religion in a great variety of ways, of which the AICs form only one—itself very diverse—type of expression. Characteristic of all types of Christian belief in Africa is their need to interact with forms of traditional belief, whether in a positive manner as do most AICs, which accommodate significant features of African indigenous beliefs, or in the negative manner characteristic of many of today's charismatic churches, which tend to reject traditional beliefs as evil. Some form of interaction with traditional forms of belief is inescapable, in that all imported religious traditions, including Christianity, are built on existing historical patterns. African traditional religions are fully part of this history.

I am using the term "African traditional religions" (ATRs) for want of a better one, and since this is how they are widely known in the literature.[13] These are religions based on oral traditions that do not have an authoritative written source. In the literature they are often referred to as primitive, primal, or pre-literate religions, or, among scholars nowadays, as traditional or oral religions. These labels have in common that they are generally applied to the religious beliefs and practices of people who are deemed to fall outside the mainstream of world history. A salient characteristic of religions of this type, compared to the inherent missionary zeal of Christianity and Islam—the two main competitors in Africa in religious terms—is their lack of motivation to broaden their appeal outside their own community. This does not mean that African traditional religions lack the ability to incorporate newcomers in the community of believers. Rather, the opposite is the case: precisely because they lack a written dogma, such religions are usually open in character, very flexible and adaptable, not only prepared to make room for others but actually offering space for this purpose. This is true in regard to people, but above all in regard to ideas. Interestingly, this trait in particular—the capacity to absorb new ideas—continues to have an impact on later arrivals on the religious scene, such as Christianity, as we will see in subsequent chapters.

The interface between traditional religion and Christianity in Africa remains one of the most challenging subjects in the life of the Church, and, as we will see, one of the most controversial ones. African notions of the spirit world and its operations; notions of evil, which include, for example, witch-craft beliefs; ideas concerning illness and healing; and notions of progress and prosperity all affect Christian thought and practice in Africa. These are not in any way unchanging, as the basic principles underlying the ideas express themselves differently in various times and places. What has hardly changed, and is not likely to change any time soon, are the principles themselves, whose main characteristic is connectedness with a spirit world.

Whereas in the past the various forms of African religious life were often seen as "superstitious" or involving forms of idolatry, some of their main characteristics may well shape much of Christian belief and practice in the twenty-first century, especially in view of African migration trends. As a re-sult of international migration, African-initiated churches can now be found all over the world.[14] One consequence of this mobility—surprising to many people in Europe—is that the original direction of the Christian mission has become reversed. Today we see Africans evangelizing in Europe, in an attempt to bring the gospel back to a continent that many Africans believe to have lost its original spiritual roots.

Tilting the Balance in the Church

The rise of new churches in Europe founded by Africans has come as a sur-prise to most churches in the West. Although prediction is difficult, it seems unavoidable that the emergence of African-initiated churches in Europe will alter the relationships between churches in Africa and Europe. After most African countries gained political independence in the 1960s, the churches in Africa, too, embarked on a process of "africanization" that gradually put con-trol in the hands of Africans, tilting the balance of power from the "mother" to the "daughter" churches, changing the relationship from a parent-child to a sibling relationship. That this is not an easy process may be illustrated with the example of Emmanuel Milingo, the former Catholic archbishop of Lusaka, Zambia, who ran into great trouble with his own Church when he started to exercise spiritual independence.[15] He was excommunicated in 2006 following his ordination of a number of married priests in the United States. Milingo had publicly associated himself with the Family Federation for World Peace and Unification, a movement originally founded in Korea by the Reverend Sun Myung Moon, and is himself now also married. These events formed the climax of a process that lasted at least twenty-five years, during which Milingo tried to convince his Church to take African spirituality seriously rather than simply patronize African Christians. Criticizing the paternalistic attitude of the Church in Europe toward Africa he has commented: "We thank her [Europe] for what she has done to us, and we appreciate her worries and anxieties about us. But we believe that she, as a grandmother to us, should now worry much more about her problems of old age, than about us."[16]

Archbishop Milingo has always been an important spokesman for the African Church, not officially, but certainly popularly. He grew to fame in the 1970s when he became known as a Christian healer, someone who could heal people from their physical and mental ailments through the power of Christ. In Zambia, many such ailments were commonly ascribed to the intrusion of evil spirits that would take control of the human body and cause havoc in the life of a person. To get rid of such harmful spirits, people would visit traditional healers, who shared popular cosmological ideas and understood the nature of these complaints. European mission churches, on the other hand, rejected the popular belief in evil spirits, which, apart from any theological considerations, implied an unacceptable rupture with the scientific type of thought that the Western-Christian Church has appropriated since the Enlightenment. Hence, the Church refused to address the life-problems of many Africans—not only in Zambia—by denying the reality of their spirit world. Archbishop Milingo, however, had no hesitation in accepting this reality once he had become aware of his gift of healing, which he accepted as a gift of God and which he therefore believed he had to put to God's service. Milingo began to heal people suffering from evil spirits by exorcising them through the power of the Holy Spirit, convincing his parishioners that there was no need for them to visit traditional healers secretly at night, since the Christian Church had free access to the greatest of all the spirits in the spirit world. Through the Holy Spirit, Milingo claimed, the power of evil spirits will be broken.

Once it had been announced that people suffering from evil spirits could be healed in the Church, people came in increasingly large numbers to the Catholic Cathedral in Lusaka. The spiritual needs of African Christians were now directly addressed, much to the annoyance of both missionaries and church prelates in Zambia. Eventually, in 1982, Milingo was called to Rome by the Vatican, where he was first kept for examination of both his physical and mental condition—some considered him to be mad—and his theological views. The term "superstition" could often be heard in this context, both in missionary circles and in the Vatican (not to speak of the numerous often rather racist comments in media in the West[17]). In every respect, however, Milingo was found to be totally sound. Nevertheless, he was never allowed to return to his post in Zambia and was given an administrative job in Rome. In obedience to the pope, John Paul II, himself known for his mystical inclination, Milingo complied. Although his own desire was to continue working in Africa, he soon appreciated the opportunities in the new circumstances of his life, as he realized that, no longer confined to Zambia, he could turn the whole world into his field of action. He came to see his work as a global mission and began to travel throughout the world to share his gift of healing with those who needed it. In effect, he became Africa's most famous missionary to the West in modern times.

It soon became clear that Milingo's gift of healing was almost as much sought after and appreciated by the public at large in the West as it had been in Africa. He grew immensely popular in Italy, where people started to flock to him as they did in Zambia. They tried to locate him at home, phoned him constantly in the office, and invited him to conduct healing services. In the meantime, both the Italian and the international press showed great interest in him, which contributed further to his fame. His success appalled Vatican officials, who had no affinity whatsoever with a worldview that focused on the spirit world, seen as a battlefield between the Holy Spirit and powers of darkness. During all the years Milingo lived in Rome, his adversaries in the Vatican did everything within their power to block his ministry. His freedom of movement was increasingly restricted as he grew in popularity, and his healing ministry became effectively hindered by the hierarchy. This was the main reason Milingo engaged himself in the past few years with the Reverend Moon and his Family Federation for World Peace and Unification. This connection opened up new avenues, as significant similarities in worldview attracted the two men to each other. The most important point of resemblance is in their cosmology, in both cases strongly influenced by their non-Western origin. They share a belief in a spirit world and in the human ability to communicate effectively with the beings that are supposed to dwell there.

Archbishop Milingo's life is in fact a good example of how difficult it appears to be to accept African views as genuine expressions of Christianity, and to adapt the balance of power in the Church to the realities of today. Although the dismissive attitude of Western Christians is no longer as widespread as it used to be, African Christians continue to have the feeling that they are required to stay in the kitchen, while others are enjoying themselves in the living room. To them it seems that to acquire the certificate of true Christianity one has to stem from a Western-Christian tradition, or otherwise adapt to it completely. But, as Milingo once put it so eloquently, "To convince me that I can only be a full Christian when I shall well be brought up in European civilization and culture, is to force me to change my nature. If God made a mistake by creating me an African, it is not yet evident. My antagonists have not yet given me summons to call me to the high court of God, where He promised to undo me as an African in order to make me a European as a process and a 'conditio sine qua non' to become a full Christian."[18]

Milingo's life story highlights the fundamental differences in cosmological understanding between (western) Europe and (sub-Saharan) Africa, where the belief in evil spirits and other manifestations of evil, such as "witches," is widespread. In Africa, religion does not represent a philosophy of life that searches for ultimate meaning,[19] as it does for many Western Christians today. Rather, it represents a view of life that acknowledges the existence of an invisible world, believed to be inhabited by spiritual forces that are deemed to have effective powers over one's life. The spirit world is considered to be distinct but not separate from the visible world of human beings. One implication of such a worldview is that the invisible world is an extension of the visible one, and people's social relations extend into it. Therefore it is important for human beings to maintain a good relationship with this spirit world.

African religious ideas, argues British historian Terence Ranger, are to a large extent ideas about relationships: relations with other human beings, with the spirits of the dead, with animals, with the land, with the forest.[20] These relationships are often expressed in terms of relations with spirits, which we may refer to as a "spirit idiom": ancestral spirits, spirits of the land, water or forest, or alien spirits. The spirit idiom is one of personification, which dramatizes the personal rather than the metaphorical aspect of relationships: it represents spirits as something real and concrete. Spirits can manifest themselves by, quite literally, taking possession of a living person (as we will see in Chapter 3). In such a case a temporary personality change takes place, during which the possessed person assumes the personality ascribed to the possessing spirit. These and other ideas pertaining to relationships, the spirit world, and spirit possession all serve to regulate the relationships between people and the rules that govern their interaction. At the same time the spirit idiom may serve as an explanatory model for illness, adversity, or other forms of misfortune, which are perceived as a rupture in the relationship between the human and the spirit world. To restore the relationship one has to identify which spirit may be causing the disturbance and needs to be propitiated in order to redress the balance.

African Religious Ideas

Apart from their spirit-oriented nature, African religious beliefs are generally characterized by a number of distinguishable traits, chief among them a preoccupation with evil or the nature of evil. In African societies, evil is a metaphysical entity that is often experienced as real, concrete, and almost tangible. It may take the form of evil spirits, but it can also be manifested through human beings in the form of witchcraft. A so-called witch is a person whom the wider community believe to manipulate mystical powers to the detriment of others, notably those closest to him or her, such as neighbors or relatives. On a different plane, such powers can also be used by politicians, including heads of state, who try to increase their political power by spiritual means.[21] Lack of understanding of the nature of power in Africa, which most Africans believe to contain an inherently spiritual component, continues to be one of the main encumbrances to relations between churches in Europe and churches in Africa; the case of Archbishop Milingo is only one telling example. The same lack of understanding also risks becoming a major obstacle in the relations between the historical mainline churches in western Europe and those founded there in recent years by Africans. Given the precarious circumstances in which many African Christians find themselves in Europe, they are also preoccupied with the need to counter evil forces, for which they call upon the power of the Holy Spirit. Here, too, the emphasis is on direct communication with the spirit world, in this case a spirit world of Christian character, through divine revelation, prophecy, wonders and miracles, healing, and possession by the Holy Spirit.

The general lack of understanding of the nature of power as it is widely perceived in Africa also explains the general neglect by Western churches of religious or spiritual healing. Spiritual healing is an essential characteristic of all religious traditions in Africa, including Christianity. The neglect of this aspect in the former mission churches has contributed enormously to the emergence of the independent churches in Africa today. In fact, the latter are often labeled by outsiders as "healing churches," highlighting a specific aspect of church life that, though normal to African believers, is clearly unfamiliar to others. When I once asked a member of the Zion Christian Church (ZCC), one of the largest independent churches in South Africa and neighboring countries, at ZCC headquarters why he had changed his Anglican membership for the ZCC, he gave a remarkably simple and clear answer. He said: "They heal you, they forgive you your sins, and they promise you eternal life," summarizing in a nutshell the most urgent spiritual needs for many African believers. The healing dimension is crucial to the well-being of individuals and communities in Africa, representing their characteristic holistic outlook on life; the emphasis on forgiveness of sins demonstrates the need to redress the balance of good and evil; and the reference to eternal life highlights how many Africans continue to attach great value to life outside the material world, that is, in the invisible world where, among others, the ancestors are believed to reside. Ancestors are good spirits, believed to protect and guide the community. When ancestral spirits turn against people, this is not to cause harm but to prevent harm from gaining a foothold in the community through the irresponsible behavior of individuals who neglect the way of the ancestors. Once the angered ancestor is propitiated, the harmonious balance of life will be restored, with the ancestral spirits resuming their normal task.

When Archbishop Milingo embarked on his healing ministry, he was clearly operating in a longstanding African religious, social, and cultural tradition. A person in good health is one who lives in balance with the rest of the universe, including the world of spirits. While this has long been neglected by churches in the West, due to their different context and history, today we see the same lack of understanding repeated in the world of development cooperation. Like their missionary predecessors, most Western development organizations consider health and healing a purely secular matter that can be resolved by technical and material means, such as access to drugs or, as in the case of AIDS, through the distribution and use of condoms. While this would certainly help, such an approach will fail to be effective if, as is already abundantly clear, it is not accompanied by an approach that takes account of the holistic worldview of most Africans in which the material and the spiritual world are bound together. The fact that many AIDS patients in Africa visit traditional healers in search of a cure cannot be ascribed solely to lack of access to a Western-trained medical doctor or a health clinic, but is also related to a need to address the spiritual dimension of sickness. The parallel with African people's response to the lack of healing in the former mission churches is a striking one.

African religious ideas are not static, though, nor have they ever been. In his sketch for a historical model of the religious history of Africa, Terence Ranger has emphasized the dynamic character of African traditional religious ideas, which leave abundant room for innovation, integration, and adaptation.[22] One significant way this has happened, I would suggest, is through their contextual interpretation by African Christians. This is noticeable particularly in the independent church tradition, which is most clear in its spirit orientation, but also increasingly outside it, through a process of charismatization of former mission churches.[23] Today, the self-confidence with which African Christians express their spiritual concerns in the latest and highly popular branch of independent churches, the charismatic churches, is indicative of the manner in which Africans continue to appropriate Christian religion in ways that suit them best.

This fact is also noticeable in the ways African spiritual ideas have been carried overseas and incorporated into the life of African Christian communities outside Africa, including in Europe, perpetuating what has sometimes been called a Black Church tradition. Significant aspects of the latter, as Walter Hollenweger has pointed out, are the orality of liturgy and the narrativity of theology; the participatory character of services and of church life more generally; the importance of dreams and visions; and the specific understanding of the body-mind relationship, which becomes particularly clear in the importance attached to healing through prayer.[24] The extreme attention to the Bible as the authoritative and infallible word of God is another notable point of distinction between African Christians and most of their Western counterparts. All these, we should note, are elements of Christianity in Africa that appear remarkable to Western believers, whose religious practice is based on, and shaped by, a different cultural tradition. To them, the widespread African belief in the presence and instrumentality of spiritual forces, whether good or evil, is perhaps the most striking difference between Western and African approaches.

Inculturation, Africanization, and Identity

It may be clear from the discussion so far that much has changed in the relationship between Europe and Africa since the onset of nineteenth-century evangelism. Not only have African Christians become increasingly independent-minded in running their religious affairs, in both thought and practice, but they even consider it their God-given task today to reconvert what former U.S. secretary of defense Donald Rumsfeld once referred to as "old" Europe, a subject I return to in Chapter 7. This throws a new light also on the question of inculturation, a much-debated issue in the Church.

The need for inculturation of Christianity, in this case in Africa, has been stressed by many, but it is not always clear what precisely is understood by it. Often, the word has been used in such a way as to suggest that the matter revolves around the question of how Christianity can be transplanted from one particular local context—in this case western Europe—to another—Africa—in such a way that it will take root there. This has often been described with the term "africanization," suggesting a form of inculturation particularly suitable for Africa. During the controversy concerning Archbishop Milingo's healing ministry, the archbishop made some interesting comments showing the limitations of the concept, inasmuch as inculturation is often seen as a single act rather than a two-way process. As he has pointed out,[25] inculturation should be understood not as unidirectional but as a process of cross-fertilization, in which different cultures enrich one another other while preserving the characteristics that make up their original identity. Genuine and fruitful inculturation will effect mutual change, or changes in both contexts: the place the idea or practice came from as well as the place to which it was taken. According to Milingo, the African continent must liberate itself from the image of an inaccessible and distant God, so alien to the tradition of direct communication with the spirit world, and demand the right to bring in its own spiritual experiences, to the enrichment of the whole Church. In other words, africanization as a specific expression of inculturation is not something peculiar to Africa which is good or relevant for Africa alone, but something that non-Africans should also benefit from. Africanization is a form of inculturation that contains a universal element. It means not only that African Christians should be allowed to express Christianity in their own way, but also that in doing so they have a specific contribution to make to the Church as a whole. The call for a healing ministry in the Church as a universal body is a pertinent example.

Recently, some anthropologists have suggested that the concept of africanization has become superfluous in modern times and should be avoided in future discussions. It has been argued that after a long period in which the research interests of anthropologists, missiologists, and theologians converged on the issue of africanization—whose common concern is stated to be the search for an "authentic African expression of Christianity"—this notion no longer makes sense.[26] This may be true from an outsider's perspective that has habitually considered africanization a specifically African concern rather than a form of inculturation that involves both parties. But it fails to consider the continuing insiders' need for recognition of the specific contribution Africa might make to Christianity as a universal religion. Since the original arrival of European missionaries in Africa, God has gradually become African, to such a degree that the change is beginning to affect the rest of the world. African-ness, or being African, is no longer a local identity only, but has become a distinctive part of a global identity.

It is worth considering the idea of African identity a bit further in this context, as it appears to be understood rather differently by African Christians and Western observers. Whereas African Christians tend to consider African identity a particular expression of human identity shaped by specific sociocultural conditions, thus allowing them a legitimate place within the global community, Western observers often seem to consider it a unique, almost innate feature that characterizes black people with roots in the African continent. In studying African communities, whether in or outside Africa, the scholarly focus is often on ethnicity and ethnic adherence, often at the expense of religious identity.

So prevalent is the study of ethnicity in modern anthropology that a leading American anthropologist, Sally Falk Moore, has wondered whether, in terms of anthropological theory, ethnicity has become the avatar of tribe.[27] Anthropologists, like other Western observers, were until quite recent times accustomed to think of Africans as forming political and social groups called "tribes," and to consider those groups a phenomenon characteristic of Africa and other parts of what would later be called the developing world. The idea, prevalent until the mid-twentieth century, that Africans lived in "tribes" that were the vehicle of their ethnic identity was also a racial one, combined with notions of hierarchy and evolution. While the concept of race is no longer scientifically respectable, and that of "tribe" is also avoided by most social scientists, ethnicity has come to enjoy wide currency. Hence African identity has become an ethnic identity, as a result of which African Christians, too, are primarily seen as Africans rather than as Christians. These observations can be equally applied to the situation of African Christians in Europe today, whose identity is often considered in similar terms. The difference between the ascribed ethnic identity of African Christians and their religious self-definition seems to confirm the argument by philosopher Charles Taylor in his book on multiculturalism and the politics of recognition, that identity is often shaped by the misrecognition of others.[28]

In due course, I will explore some specific aspects of African Christian identity. As I have suggested, crucial to it is the way in which African believers consider the spirit world, a topic to be discussed in the following chapter.

Chapter Three
The African Spirit World:
A Journey into the Unknown

In Africa, religion generally refers to a belief in the existence of an invisible world, distinct but not separate from the visible one, which is home to spiritual beings with effective powers over the material world. Although this is by no means unique to Africa, such an understanding of what religion actually *is*, is often not compatible with the religious understanding of mainstream Christians in western Europe, which has been shaped by different social and historical experiences as well as by a distinct intellectual tradition. Unlike probably most Western Christians, African Christians believe in the reality of a spirit world, with which they may interact freely and frequently, according to circumstances.

In the following pages I discuss in particular one of the most important ways in which African believers have traditionally managed their relations with the spirit world, spirit possession, and how this type of interaction has been affected by the introduction of Christian religion. One of the consequences of the missionary endeavor in Africa has been the disruption of the traditional religious mechanisms by which individuals and communities could accommodate the various forms of evil they experienced in their lives, such as illness, death, and other forms of human misery. In fact, the disappearance of such traditional mechanisms has been identified as one of the main reasons for the current need of a ministry of deliverance within the Church in Africa.[1]

The Nature of the Spirit World

There is an extensive body of literature concerning African spirit beliefs or "African religion" more generally, authored by both Africans and non-Africans. In the history of academic writing on religion in Africa, two successive phases can be distinguished.[2] The first is characterized by an "Africa as object" approach, referring to an early period in which religious data were studied by scholars from outside Africa, many of them amateur ethnographers. The second is characterized by an "Africa as subject" approach, when similar data are also being studied by professionally trained specialists, including African scholars based in African universities. Accompanying this change of phase from Africa-as-object to Africa-as-subject was a change in the moral value that observers ascribed to religion in Africa. The history of this change has been recorded in more recent academic works.[3]

With due consideration for the great diversity of the spirit world as traditionally experienced by many Africans, the picture arising from the various descriptions shows certain commonalities. The African spirit world can generally be said to be inhabited by all kinds of invisible beings, pretty much similar to the great variety of human beings in the visible world: they are of different types and are different in individual character. The moral nature of spirits traditionally depended largely on the quality of the relationship between the human and spirit world. For a prosperous and stable life, many Africans believe, humans need to maintain a good relation with the spirit world. This requires regular attention, as do all social relations in the human world. If the relationship is well maintained, the spirits will be content and placid; if not, they will attract attention to themselves by causing trouble. People may seek good offices from a particular spirit, for example for protection, but may also want malevolent services, with a view to harming others. In particular, no decision of any importance would be taken without consulting relevant spirits. Ideas about the workings of the spirit world in their relations with human beings can be found in great variety in all parts of Africa, and can be observed in the works of African writers, including African novelists such as Ben Okri and Amos Tutuola.[4] They can also be found in the popular pamphlets and videos that are sold at markets and other places where people meet on a regular basis and exchange ideas.[5] The impact of ideas about the spirit world is equally apparent from the importance of widespread practices of divination, an umbrella term referring to a great variety of techniques for influencing decisions in the spirit world. Through divination, individuals may literally dis-cover (uncover what is hidden) what the spirits hold in store for them, as they alone know humans' real destination in life. Hence, divination becomes a way to keep one's life on course with the help of the spirit world. It is the spiritual aspect of the human person that is believed to connect him or her to that world.

Although African ideas concerning the existence of a spirit world have undergone little basic change, the believed nature of that world is not the same as it used to be. In recent years, attention has been drawn to the way the traditional spirit world has become demonized under the influence of Christianity, with the effect that appellations of the devil have entered the spiritual vocabulary. There is now a common belief among African Christians that Satan is the main source of suffering and as such the greatest enemy of humankind.[6] Perhaps the best way to explore this change is through the views of Zambian Archbishop Milingo (to whom I have referred before), controversial in the West but famous in Africa as a Christian healer. When he became archbishop of Lusaka in 1969, he continued to show the same concern for the daily problems of his parishioners as he had during his earlier career as a parish priest. The dramatic confrontation referred to in Chapter 1 marked the beginning of his healing ministry. Milingo became convinced that as a prelate of the Church he had to become a servant of the people, and that he could best do this by invoking the power of the Holy Spirit to liberate those who suffer from evil spirits.[7] He discovered that many Zambians lived in a state of spiritual confusion, and he therefore set out to help them develop a new vision of the cosmic order, in which the terror of evil spirits could be countered by the power of the Holy Spirit. His sensitivity to the spiritual needs of Africans caused his reputation as an effective Christian healer to spread.

In many African countries, people's cosmic vision, formerly a balanced one, has been thrown into disequilibrium, creating a world in which evil can no longer be accommodated. The reasons for this situation are complex. The neutral character that Africans traditionally ascribe to the spirit world has changed dramatically under the influence of Christianity. The result is that many people can no longer accommodate angered spirits by propitiating them, but must drive them out since they have come to be seen as inherently evil. Whereas an angered spirit may resume its neutral position, an evil spirit cannot be expected to change its fundamental nature. Hence, as a bishop and pastor, Milingo's exorcisms were aimed at establishing a new order in the religious havoc that had been created in many people's minds as a result of the Church's rejection of their traditional religious views. This he did by demarcating the spheres of good and evil in the spirit world, trying "to unshackle and make free what its missionary priests had unwittingly bound."[8] Exorcism became thus a necessary, liberating phase in the healing process. The experience of evil also explains the popularity in Africa today of neopentecostal and charismatic churches, which consider the fight against evil forces one of their main tasks and responsibilities. In fact, the fight against evil, in whatever form or shape it may manifest itself, has become a major attraction for any new religious movement in Africa as well as among Africans in the diaspora.

Archbishop Milingo has set out his ideas about the spirit world in a series of writings about his healing ministry that incorporate insights from the traditional spirit world of Zambians.[9] Not only is he a prolific writer, but his practical experience regarding the perceived spirit world has few equals. His decision, as archbishop of Lusaka, to take the African spirit world seriously, where the Church hierarchy refused to recognize its reality, led him on a personal journey to explore the traditional beliefs and practices of Zambian people. Since his first experience of the power of the Holy Spirit in 1973, he has continually had spiritual experiences through dreams and visions. These started shortly after that first encounter, when he was attending a course in Rome, studying documents of the Second Vatican Council. As he was reading in bed, he saw something like a shadow approaching him and covering him completely till he found himself in a state of transformation. He then heard a voice telling him "to go and preach the gospel," which he came to explain as an instruction to use his healing gift as part of the evangelizing mission of the Church. During a visit in 2006 he recalled the event to me once again, as well as sharing with me some of his latest encounters in the spirit world.

In Milingo's view, the spirit world can best be described as a world in-between, the dwelling place of a great variety of spiritual beings. It forms a point of contact and a place of mediation between the human world and the world of God, a place where the spheres of earth and heaven meet. The world in-between is the abode of the ancestors and other protective spirits. However, it is also the home of evil spirits whose presence is equally real and whose influence is considerable. They may be held responsible for all sorts of trouble in different spheres of life. Evil spirits are believed to be bad by nature, and therefore they cannot be accommodated, in contrast to other spirits, such as ancestors, whose attitude and behavior depend on the quality and nature of their relationship with human beings. Evil spirits have to be driven away, and no compromises can be made with them. At the same time, the world in-between is seen as containing the ability to transform human beings, either for good or for evil. In the latter case—the reasoning goes—humans will ally themselves with the devil; in the former, they will live a godly life that is empowered by the Holy Spirit. It is in this world in-between, according to Milingo, that the final decisions are made that govern the fate of individual human beings. Hence, the type and quality of communication with the spirit world are of crucial importance and, from an African Christian perspective, should not be left to non-Christians alone (such as traditional healers).

The idea that decisions affecting life on earth are made outside the visible sphere of the cosmos, reflects the relative importance that many Africans attribute to the spirit world. From this it also follows that it is of the greatest importance for people to have some form of effective communication with this invisible world, since this is believed to be the place where the key decisions about their lives are taken. One important means of communication with the spirit world in Africa is through spirit possession.

Spirit Possession: What Is It?

A journey into the spirit world is like a journey into the unknown, as a traveler from the human world is acting under the influence of an external spiritual force. Milingo has described how, in such a state, his body feels calm and relaxed, as he has the sensation of loss of weight and physical feeling. In fact, he says, his body feels as though it is acting under the influence of an external power, while his will and mind remain under his own control.[10] Since a journey into the spirit world is considered to be not without risk (as will be seen in the next chapter), it requires spiritual preparation in such a way that the evil forces that might be waiting to attack will be rendered harmless. Only the spiritually strongest people may return from the spirit world unharmed. Known as spirit mediums, they become mediators for others, who are less spiritually gifted, conveying messages from the spirit world to them.

Spirit mediumship is a well-known phenomenon in Africa, and there is a wide literature on it. Spirit mediums are generally important and respected members of the community who enjoy great social prestige. They are believed to have been chosen by a benevolent spirit to act as mediums in order to bring important messages from the spirit world to the local community or certain of its members. In such cases, the invisible spirit is believed to take possession of the person in such a way that his or her body becomes a vehicle for the spirit. Spirit possession thus opens up a field of communication with a world beyond ordinary human experience, where invisible beings can influence the lives of their human counterparts for good or ill. When possession takes place, the person is no longer considered his or her normal self, but in the view of believers *becomes* the spirit for the duration of the possession. Depending on the identity of the spirit that is believed to have taken possession, spirit mediums will speak and act in ways associated with the particular spirit, which are often quite different from their own normal behavior. This is the case not only with spirit mediums, but also with people who are possessed by evil spirits. They may speak with completely different voices that are ascribed to the spirit believed to have taken possession of them, and they demonstrate a radical change in their bodily behavior.[11] In such cases, the spirit presence is experienced as malevolent and harmful, and the only remedy becomes exorcism. This is precisely what Milingo took upon himself and what led him into serious trouble with the Catholic Church.

Spirit possession is a phenomenon that also occurs in the Bible, in various forms. The New Testament provides numerous examples of people possessed by evil spirits, demons, or Satan, and in need of deliverance. Jesus himself is frequently described as an exorcist.[12] But the Bible also describes forms of possession by the Holy Spirit, such as on the day of Pentecost. In the Christian tradition a clear distinction is usually made between possession by evil spirits, such as Satan, on the one hand, and by good spirits, such as the Holy Spirit, on the other. This is typical of religions that are characterized by an ethical dualism, recognizing a stark contrast between good and evil. This includes Christianity. Hence, an equally stark contrast is made between possession by an absolutely good spirit being (such as the Holy Spirit) and an absolutely evil one (such as Satan or other demons). In case of the latter, exorcism is recommended. This clear distinction between what Christian believers perceive as good and evil forms of possession is also expressed in the terms they use to describe the phenomenon. While the term "spirit possession" or just "possession" is usually exclusively reserved to refer to evil spirits, when it concerns the Holy Spirit, the Christian spirit of absolute good, a different terminology is used. This may be seen in the Bible, where the Holy Spirit "comes down" on people (Mk 1:10) or "alights" on them (Mt. 3:16), or they are "filled" with the Holy Spirit (Acts 2:4). Thus, today, charismatic believers may refer to the "in-dwelling" of the Holy Spirit, a term they would not use to describe the believed presence of an evil spirit in a person. In most religions, however, no such sharp contrast is made between good and evil spirits. The invisible beings, or spirits, are considered amoral; being good or evil is not an inherent aspect of their character, but depends on the relationship between the invisible beings and those who believe in their existence. Such is also traditionally the case in Africa. In contrast to most Western societies, in Africa there is normally no negative connotation attached to spirit possession.

Neurobiological Aspects of Spirit Possession

Spirit possession is not something peculiar to Africa. It is in fact a common religious phenomenon in most parts of the world. Modern Western society appears exceptional in this regard. In the West generally, spirit possession has a bad name. It has often been seen, and still is in many cases, as a mental disorder, a psychiatric condition that should be treated within the biomedical framework developed for such dysfunction. Such a framework does not allow for an alternative interpretation in terms derived from the specific history and intellectual tradition in which spirit possession occurs. Yet, the comparison with certain psychiatric conditions known in the West may shed some light on the neurophysiological basis of the phenomenon. Felicitas Goodman, an American anthropologist who has done extensive research on spirit possession, including through experiments, has made a comparison between the condition of, say, an African possessed by a spirit and a Westerner, say, an American, suffering from a multiple or split personality syndrome. Characteristic of both states is the ability to exhibit several different personalities, which the subjects/actors experience as existing inside them. It has been established that observable changes take place in the brains of persons with a multiple personality syndrome, altering their "brain map" in such a way as to give rise to an alternate personality. A similar type of neurophysiological change of the brain is believed to take place during spirit possession.[13] In other words, the neurophysiological characteristics are the same, whether for an African, an American, or a European.

There is one vital difference, however, which is located outside the individual afflicted: societies that culturally approve of spirit possession submit it to ritual control, which is not the case with behavior seen as psychiatric disorder. This explains why possession behavior in Africa is not, and should not be seen as, a form of mental disorder. It is a type of controlled behavior that constitutes a manipulation of brain processes that can actually be learned. Spirit mediums go through a long period of training under the guidance of an experienced medium, a process that can take many years. The possibility also exists of possession by an unruly spirit, as is believed to be the case in demonic possession. The latter, however, normally happens not to a spirit medium but rather to ordinary believers, who therefore need the services of a medium to deal with the situation. Archbishop Milingo, for example, had become such a medium, in this case of the Holy Spirit, to fight the evil spirits that so many African Christians felt to afflict them, and to liberate people from their oppression.

Goodman conceives of the issue in terms of a continuum that extends from learned and ritually controlled possession at one end to demonic possession or multiple personality disorder at the other. In societies such as those of Africa, where spirit beliefs are part of people's cosmologies, exorcism constitutes a form of ritual control over demonic possession, which opens the way to healing for the person troubled by it. Looked at this way, the work of someone like Archbishop Milingo takes on quite a different significance from that usually ascribed to it by elite religious circles in the West. The clue to his success as a healer lies in the apparent possibility of producing a change in the brain map of the sufferer by the use of trance. Goodman refers in this regard to the exorcist as the supreme "turner," "the one who is called on to wipe the injurious map off the slate, so that health may be restored."[14]

Possession behavior is trance behavior, which can be learned, since people all over the world share the neurophysiological characteristics that may give rise to such behavior. In other words, spirit possession is a type of behavior that is based on a universal human potentiality. Obviously this will only be activated in a cultural setting that is conducive to displaying such behavior. This is generally not the case in western Europe, where social respect is derived from the ability to retain self-control under all circumstances, in contrast to African societies, where, as we have seen, social prestige is often accorded to those with an ability to open themselves up to external forces that may temporarily take over control. Goodman has explained the difference by making the following analogy. In societies where spirit possession is accepted behavior, a human being can be likened to a car with a driver. The car is the body and the driver the soul. Just as the driver sets the car in motion, so the soul is believed to activate the body. On occasion the owner may invite a friend with no car temporarily to take over the wheel and drive. Something similar happens in spirit possession, where an entity with no physical body of its own is invited to enter the medium's body and temporarily takes over control.[15] This may be the spirit of an ancestor, a deity, or even an animal. It may also be the Holy Spirit.

For a long time, the Western biomedical paradigm and non-Western soul theories developed in opposite directions, but recent developments show some degree of convergence. In part, this is due to a growing interest in the West in charismatic types of belief, but it is also a consequence of new scientific developments concerning the workings of the brain.[16] A brief elaboration of the neurobiological aspects of spirit possession is also important in view of the wider discussion in our secularized societies concerning the continuing interest of many people in religion. Once again, there appears to be a common neurobiological basis for such an interest, one that may or may not be activated, depending on the type of society in which one lives. Neurobiological research in the late 1990s suggests the presence in the human brain of what is popularly referred to as the "God spot," a mass of neural tissue in the brain's temporal lobes (located just behind the temples) that is considered responsible for enabling human beings to have a sense of the sacred and a consciousness of deeper things in life. The "God spot" is considered to permit the presence of religious ideas and practices in the form of rites and rituals. This, reportedly, is the part of the brain that is active when people have spiritual experiences such as those mentioned (and of the sort discussed in more detail in the next chapter). Scientific experiments carried out with the help of magnetic sensors registered strong magnetic activity in the brain's temporal lobes when the subjects thought—as they had been asked to do—about whatever was sacred to them.[17] It has been suggested that—although not fully or uniquely—the "God spot" is also the basis of a spiritual intelligence that is apt to promote the quality of life, a subject I will return to in Chapter 6. *Intelligent* spiritual experience (because the same part of the brain appears highly active in borderline schizophrenics, for example) must be fully integrated with wider brain activity.

The study of the neural basis of spirituality is of course not undisputed, particularly since modern science is based on an almost exclusively materialist interpretation of reality. There are new branches of study, however, that attempt to explore new paths to understanding neglected fields of human experience, applying insights from modern science to areas of life that had previously been delegated to the domain of theology and therefore declared irrelevant to modern science. One such branch of study, known somewhat misleadingly as "neurotheology," a term originating in Aldous Huxley's novel *Island*, seeks to investigate the relationship between spirituality and the brain. The term neurotheology is particularly unfortunate as it is not only used by scholars but has also been adopted by non-academics to represent specific religious perspectives. Neurotheology explores the neurological and evolutionary basis for subjective experiences that are often categorized as "spiritual," a blanket term for a great variety of human phenomena that cannot—or not yet—be explained by the methods of conventional natural science.

One of the pioneers in this new area of study is Andrew Newberg, who, with others, has introduced the concept of neurotheology to describe the scientific study of spiritual experiences.[18] Newberg, a medical specialist, is only one of several modern scientists who take seriously the possibility of developing a scientific paradigm that is not exclusively based on a materialist worldview. He is the director of the first university research center in the United States that focuses on the relationship between spirituality and the human brain, the Center for Spirituality and the Mind at the University of Pennsylvania. Such scientific research, in combination with certain social developments, notably international migration, may well bring two formerly exclusive paradigms—the biomedical and the "soul" theory—closer together. The presence of many people in the West originating from non-Western societies has already influenced, for example, healing practices in the West. On the other hand, as we notice today, Westerners may react by sheltering themselves even more than before from "nonscientific" or spiritual influences.

Human Encounters with the Spirit World

While a healthy skepticism remains important, particularly when metaphysical claims are involved, it remains equally important to continue scientific explorations of the human mind that may help explain the type of experiences that have such a dramatic impact on the lives of many religious believers. This is notably the case concerning non-Western parts of the world, where people's ideas are rooted in historical and intellectual traditions different from those of the West, and where people have learned to acquire knowledge in various ways. One example, taken from South Africa, may illustrate the point.

In his book, *My Traitor's Heart*, white South African writer and former crime reporter Rian Malan relates the story of Simon, nicknamed the "Hammerman."[19] Searching for the deeper motives behind the terrible violence in the country in the 1980s, when the country was still under apartheid, Malan attended the court appearance of the Hammerman, who was sentenced to death for the murder of a number of white people. His nickname had been derived from the instrument he used for his killings. During the trial, it became clear that Simon Mpungose (his real name) had foreseen in a dream everything that happened to him, and that he had understood his dream as a communication from the invisible world concerning his destiny; he could not escape this fate since it had been determined in the spirit world. This is his story.

At the time of the events that gave rise to his eventual legal conviction, Simon Mpungose was a young Zulu man who had been imprisoned in South Africa's most notorious prison, Barberton in East Transvaal, for stealing a loaf of bread. He was made to do forced labor in the quarries under the most inhumane conditions while subjected to constant brutality. Under these conditions, Simon had a dream that turned out to be prophetic. In his dream, he saw himself swelling to enormous proportions, needing only to flex his muscles to make the walls of his prison crumble like the walls of Jericho. The white warders fire on him but the bullets pass through without harming him. Simon crushes the warders like insects and rolls away through the landscape like a thunderstorm, obliterating the whites in his path. In that state, he encounters a figure of overwhelming power whom he identifies as one of his persecutors. The man is faceless, but looks like the rocks he has to break with his hammer every day. Therefore, Simon kills him. After he has killed his victim in the dream, Simon is taken away and finds himself small again, shrunk back to his normal size. Driven by what he took to be a prophecy from the spirit world, revealed in his dream, Simon Mpungose later beat to death a number of white people. He hit them with a hammer, as in his dream.

Dreams are very important in the traditional religion of the Zulu, as they are in other African traditional religions. They cannot be ignored with impunity. Accordingly, Simon Mpungose took his dream to be a message from the ancestors regarding his destiny. He knew he could not ignore such a message from the spirit world but, realizing the frightful implications, he tried to escape from it. He even converted to Christianity in an attempt to stop his dream from coming true, but in vain. When after some years he was released from prison and tried to earn a living as a manual laborer, a white employer deliberately tore up his pass—a vital document in South Africa under apartheid—before his eyes. His dream came back to him, and he knew that all his efforts to run away from it had not worked and that he had to fulfill his vocation. Altogether, twelve years had passed between the dream and its realization. It had taken him twelve years to realize the impossibility of ignoring his dream. On being sentenced to death, he believed that he had at last been freed from his torment, as had been foretold in his dream. He accepted his destiny, for which he had to pay with his own life. On 20 November 1985 Simon Mpungose was hanged in the Central Prison in Pretoria.

The story of Simon is a moving account of a profound spiritual experience of a sort that is commonly found among African Christians. Take the example of Mary Akatsa, a well-known preacher and healer in Kawangware, one of the largest slums of Nairobi, where thousands of people come to seek her spiritual advice. Mary Akatsa's claims to have died and been resurrected are readily accepted by her audiences, who ascribe great spiritual authority to her on the basis of this experience. Her personal history shows distinctive features similar to those of other religious healers in Africa, who often claim to have died after serious illness and subsequently to have returned to life charged by God with a special task. This is typical of vocation stories of founders of independent churches in Africa. The content of the alleged message, too, shows remarkable similarities. There is often a moral element, exhorting people to turn to God, connected with the task of healing the sick and casting out devils. Mary Akatsa, too, was told to return to earth, heal the sick, and cast out devils while preaching the gospel. Many cases of healing are ascribed to her as the instrument of God, sometimes performed simply by touching people with the Bible. [20] For African Christians, the Bible is a rich source of inspiration in this respect. In the Old Testament healing stories are often linked to the role of prophets. We may particularly think of Elisha, who not only could heal (as in the story of Naaman, the commander of the Syrian army), but is also known as a reviver of the dead (as described in the Book of Kings). In the New Testament, the miraculous healings attributed to Jesus have created a new and dominant paradigm in African Christianity of Jesus as the Great Healer.[21]

A journey into the spirit world is perceived to be dangerous and frightening if it is not guided. This has been well understood by the independent churches in Africa, which typically pay due regard to communication with the spirit world and accommodate traditional beliefs related with it. It is notable that the Simon the Hammerman, whose story is related above, even converted to Christianity in order to escape his destiny, though to no avail. Thousands of Zambian Christians turned to the Church in vain to find an escape from torment by evil spirits, until Archbishop Milingo began to respond to their spiritual needs. We may also consider in this respect the spiritual consequences of modern wars in Africa, where spirit ideas have often played a central role. In recent years these have become widely known through international media reports from conflict areas such as Liberia and Sierra Leone, with pictures of young fighters wearing protective amulets, or through information about spirit-based movements such as the Lord's Resistance Army in Uganda. [22] The need for the reintegration of child soldiers who are guilty of the most horrendous crimes draws attention to the importance of spiritual healing, a task for which the traditional mainline churches seem ill equipped.

In Europe, too, most African Christians turn to African-initiated congregations to find spiritual healing for whatever problems they may experience in their new homeland. Spiritual healing is a form of religious healing in which the spirit idiom prevails. It is an outstanding characteristic of old and new types of African-initiated churches, as it is of many new religious movements in Africa, which practice healing methods that resonate with traditional ideas of sickness and other manifestations of evil.

In the next chapter, I continue this journey into the African spirit world by discussing the profound impact of African religious experiences on those who are subject to them.

Chapter Four
African Religious Experiences: From Suffering to Salvation

Let us delve farther into the African spirit world by discussing some crucial aspects of it that also have great impact on the way in which African Christians experience their faith, and that often lead to misunderstanding among their fellow Christians in the West. This particularly concerns the importance of miracles, visions, and dreams, all of which happen to have a prominent place in the Bible, both Old and New Testaments, with which African Christians invariably identify. Here, too, the interconnectedness of the human and spirit worlds can have a dramatic effect on the lives of individuals, often for the benefit of their communities. One who is called by the spirit, in a way described in the previous chapter, takes on a social responsibility comparable to that of the Old Testament prophets.[1]

Due to their historical worldview, African Christians are familiar with the idea of a calling. Whoever studies the religious history of the continent will be struck by the importance of this fact in all religious traditions, not just Christianity. A certain pattern can be discerned. First comes the calling to a particular office, which is then followed by an—often prolonged—period of training. A religious calling often marks the beginning of a period of agony that, on acceptance of the vocation, unfolds from an ominous beginning to a redeeming end. The unfolding path may last for a shorter or longer time, but in all cases the sufferer can be confident of the final result. The one who has been called becomes a divine messenger, and people will listen to him or her as a medium of the invisible world, the world of spirits, or the world of God. So it is in Africa's indigenous religions, but the importance attached to such profound experience is perpetuated in the religious traditions that were subsequently imported to Africa, including Christianity. Here the one who is chosen by the spirit can identify him- or herself with the agony in the garden of Gethsemane of Jesus, whose path of suffering, biblically speaking, ended in an act of salvation.

The Lord in Action

"The Lord in action" is a phrase taken from a South African clergyman[2] to describe religious experiences of the sort discussed in the previous section. Experiences like these are at the heart of the growth and flourishing of African Christianity, in the first instance on the African continent itself but also outside it. Most of the African independent churches in and outside the continent emerged as the result of a divine calling. Hence, their founding leaders are often seen as prophets. They have gone through the experience that "God's yes was louder than my no,"[3] and are therefore considered to act not on their own initiative but on the authority of a stronger power. As we will see, it is interesting to note how such perceived spiritual power may undermine the political authorities of the day. This has occurred in very many societies, at various historical periods. The Christians of the Roman empire, for example, were persecuted because they were perceived as challenging state authority, not by political action, but through their spiritual beliefs. Spiritual power, in other words, is often perceived by outsiders as *subversive* power, which, as history has often shown, even has the capacity to overcome the power of politically repressive regimes.

A good example of the process just described is the prophet Simon Kimbangu, founder of one of the largest independent churches of Africa, the Church of Jesus Christ on Earth Through the Prophet Simon Kimbangu, popularly known as the Kimbanguist Church. Originating in the early twentieth century in what was then the Belgian Congo, the church rapidly spread to other African countries as well as outside the continent, notably the United States and Europe. Kimbangu's life story is illustrative of the profound religious experiences to which African believers are in principle open. In 1918, when the catastrophic global influenza epidemic was ravaging the country, Kimbangu received for the first time what he believed to be a divine call, a voice from the spirit world. The voice told him to go and witness Christ, and convert his brethren. Night after night the voice—believed to be of Christ himself—returned, but Kimbangu refused to obey. He fled from the village where he lived to the city, miles away, in an attempt to escape this burden, but to no avail, as the voice of Christ caught up with him wherever he went. It took him three years to realize that he could not escape his fate, and he returned to the village. Then, one day, on his way to the market, he felt pushed by invisible forces to enter the home of a woman who was ill. He laid hands on her. At that moment he experienced the power of Christ through prayer, and the woman was healed. In the eyes of the local people a miracle had occurred. Many more miracles were to follow, from miraculous healings to raising the dead.[4] Thus, after years of denial, Kimbangu eventually accepted his calling and started to work among his fellow people in the name of Christ. The people of Congo received him as a prophet and a messenger of Christ, someone sent by God for the well-being of humankind.

Characteristic of the pattern of vocations, Kimbangu's claim to act in the name and on the authority of Christ and the immense popular support for his claim—without which no prophet would last long—soon brought him into trouble with the colonial rulers, who accused him of subversion. This marked the beginning of a period of persecution and oppression of Kimbangu and his followers, in which the political authorities had the support of European missionaries. Large-scale arrests and deportations took place. Following the biblical example of Jesus, Kimbangu voluntarily surrendered to his oppressors. In October 1921, only six months after his first miraculous experience, he was condemned to 120 lashes for sedition and hostility toward whites and subsequently sentenced to death. However, King Albert of Belgium commuted the death sentence to life imprisonment. Simon Kimbangu stayed in prison for thirty years (longer than Nelson Mandela's stay on Robben Island!), until his death. Only for a short period, shorter than that of his faith model Jesus of Nazareth, had he been able to spread his message of salvation, but the effect has been lasting. The church that bears his name today counts millions of members in and outside Africa. It is one of the few African independent churches admitted to membership of the World Council of Churches.

Simon Kimbangu is only one of many prophets in the African independent churches, though perhaps the most famous one in the religious history of the continent. Famous prophets include well-known names from other parts of the continent, such as Frederick Modise of South Africa, William Wade Harris of Liberia, and others. Like Simon Kimbangu, they became known for their healing powers and even their capacity to raise the dead. Among African prophets there are many whose capacities are believed to reach beyond the borders of life, as many of them are believed to have died and risen again from the dead preceding their vocation. African prophets find ample support for their miraculous healing activities in the New Testament, where Jesus serves as the perfect example. This is all the more so as his perceived mission on earth seems directly connected with human suffering in both physical and spiritual terms. Healing being one of the central functions of religion in Africa, it marks the prophet as a real envoy of God, who shares in the anxieties of his people and is at the same time deeply involved in alleviating their suffering. In other words, not only do prophets emerge by popular acclamation, but this is actually indispensable for their functioning as charismatic leaders. This fact could be restated in sociological terms by saying that charisma is an attributed quality which can only exist in relation to others, and that, therefore, popular recognition is essential for its social functioning.

In order to understand the way many Africans experience their faith, it is of vital importance to try to understand the nature of their spiritual experiences. This is also important because of the presence of so many African Christians today in Europe, whose expressions of faith are equally characterized by a self-evident interaction with an invisible world.[5] Often the spiritual authority African prophets derive from their experiences has led to the foundation of a new church or church movement. This not only has been the case with the emergence of independent churches in the past, but is also a determining factor today in the growth of new religious movements. Healing remains central to the work of a church or group founded as a result of such an experience. The first African-initiated church in the Netherlands, for example, the True Teachings of Christ's Temple, in Amsterdam, stands in a similar spiritual tradition. Like Simon Kimbangu, its founder, Daniel Himmans-Arday, originally from Ghana, responded to a divine call and is considered a prophet. During a prolonged and mysterious illness, when every hope of recovery seemed gone and, in his own experience, his spirit had already reached the land of the dead, he had a vision that he himself recorded as follows:

[For] that night I saw the heavens opened, and there appeared twelve men in a huge basket with each holding a Holy Bible with their names written on their chests. A voice in their midst shouted, "Daniel, your salvation is at hand. I am here to heal you and then send you away to bring home all lost souls. As many as those whom you will be inspired to contact they will see salvation and here are your instructions: 'Abide by Matt. 10: 7–10 all your life and you as well as those touched to come to you will see wonders upon wonders in your lives.'"[6]

Himmans recovered and followed his vocation, as summarized in chapter 10 of the gospel of Matthew. He went out into the world to preach the gospel and heal, and, as stipulated in the same passage, without payment. It is yet another example of a typical African pattern of religious vocation: a path that leads from suffering to salvation. His personal healing experience laid the foundation of a new church.

It may be tempting to suggest that such spirit-oriented belief is limited to people who, from a European perspective, are situated outside mainstream

Christianity. This is clearly not the case, as spiritual experiences of the "from suffering to salvation" type have been recorded from various Christian quarters. We may take an example from South Africa, at the time when it was still under apartheid, in the person of Rev. Dr. Tshenuwani Simon Farisani, a dean of the Evangelical Lutheran Church and a well-known opponent of apartheid. He recorded his experiences in the form of diary notes, in which he describes his several periods in jail between 1977 and 1982 as a stay in the depths of hell.[7] Severely tortured, he received several visions that convinced him that God's power was manifesting itself and would break the hold of his enemies. One of these evoked Jesus' experiences with the powers of evil as recorded in the gospel of Luke. When in a vision Farisani encountered two large white (!) snakes in his path, towering over him and trying to bite his head, an invisible power caused them to become feeble and faint. Then a voice said (as in Lk. 10): "Listen! I have given you authority, so that you can walk on snakes and scorpions and overcome all the power of the Enemy, and nothing will hurt you." In his book Farisani compares his miraculous experiences with biblical accounts of divine salvation, such as Israel's deliverance from the hands of the Egyptian pharaoh.

Christian Miracles

"Miracle" is at bottom a religious concept. In secular terms it can be defined as something that is believed to find its origin in a dimension different from the human one. The Oxford English Dictionary describes a miracle as "a marvellous event exceeding the known powers of nature, and therefore supposed to be due to the special intervention of the Deity or of some supernatural agency; chiefly an act (e.g., healing) exhibiting control over the laws of nature, and serving as evidence that the agent is either divine or is specially favoured by God."[8] As we will see below, the two major characteristics—sign and proof—of biblical miracles appear in this classic definition. We may also note that healing is singled out as an important field of miracle working, which is particularly relevant to Africa, where both the Old and New Testament provide a rich source of inspiration and legitimation.[9]

Examining the religious history of Africa for the last hundred years, that is, since Christianity took root on the continent on a large scale, reveals numerous miracle stories that have been handed down orally or, more recently, recorded in books or, even more often, reported in the press. We are informed about healing, apparitions and revelations, stigmata, resurrection from the dead, and even virgin birth. It has sometimes been suggested that belief in miracles has revived in recent years due to the spread of neopentecostal or charismatic movements. Christian influence on miraculous events in Africa has long been significant, and it may well be that this has increased with the emergence of spiritual groups that explicitly allow for miracle working, such as healing and other acts usually ascribed to the instant effect of divine intervention.

It is clear that for African believers spiritual experiences are a source of power and inspiration that they can hardly imagine other people might leave untapped. African Christians believe in God's miraculous power. Miracles in Africa, and among African Christians outside Africa, are seen as proof of an unexpected, divine intervention—always positive—in the life of human beings. Like dreams and visions, miraculous experiences are profound religious experiences that touch on the essence of human existence, as they often concern matters of life and death. A "miracle" becomes socially significant when it is seen as a sign or proof of God's liberating power that breaks through the oppressive forces of humans and their political systems. This is the case in Europe, for example, when the immigration police, after months of delay, provide a residence permit, or when a migrant is unexpectedly set free after months in detention in anticipation of deportation. African Christians interpret these events as divine intervention, in a way that reminds them of the miraculous liberation of St. Paul from the prison in Philippi (Acts 16: 23–40). When such miraculous events happen, they testify in church, to encourage others and give thanks to the Lord to whom they ascribe this turn of fate. Hence, the phrase "Praise the Lord" can be frequently heard in their churches. Western Christians often consider this no more than a simple and somewhat naive expression of faith, because they are unable to see the important connection for African believers between spirituality and social reality. Here, too, the link between the visible and invisible worlds that forms the heart of African spirituality becomes clear. It is a spirituality that acknowledges and respects the mystery typical of African expressions of faith generally.

African Christians do not doubt God's miraculous power or healing ability. They believe in the power of prayer, which gives them unmediated access to a God who listens to them and answers their requests, a God who communicates directly with believers, perpetuating a tradition of direct communication with the spirit world. This God allows believers to share in his power by accessing the power of the Holy Spirit. Stories about such events abound in Africa, as they do among African Christians in Europe. The question whether such stories are "real," whether the events related in them "really" happened—that is, whether there is a causality relation that can be tested in a scientific-rational manner—is irrelevant in this respect. A practical approach to the subject is an actor-oriented perspective that takes personal experience as its point of departure. It is another way of saying that when a person believes, or when people believe, a miracle to have taken place, one assumes that it has indeed taken place. The question whether the miracle *really* happened may be theologically interesting but is socially irrelevant. What counts is that there are people who believe a miracle happened and who have experienced its effects.

A much more sensible question, then, is what are the effects of such a religious belief. This is a question to which Western science does actually provide an answer. Various universities, notably in the United States, itself a breeding place for charismatic belief, have (perhaps for that reason) done experimental research into the relation between the belief in faith healing and actual healing.[10] The results appear so encouraging that cynics have suggested that new horizons are opening up for secular governments to reduce the costs of health services. In sociological terms faith in God appears to be an effective strategy to promote individuals' well-being, and this observation finds increasing support from science. From that perspective, we may ascribe more rational behavior to African Christians than to many of their Western counterparts, among whom religious experiences are often met with skepticism or outright disbelief.

Christian miracles abound in Africa. Since both Old and New Testaments serve as models for many African Christians to account for their belief in miracles, it is proper to consider the specific meaning of the concept of miracle in the Bible. In the Old Testament, a miracle appears to be characterized by two things.[11] First, most miracles seem to disobey the rules of creation, bringing about a change in the order of creation by breaking through its barriers. Examples are food coming from heaven (manna), a sea being turned into dry land (the Sea of Reeds), or heavenly bodies deviating from their course. Second, certain events appear to be of a miraculous nature because they take place at precisely the right time as the result of a divine intervention. Examples are the story of Abraham who is about to sacrifice his son, Samuel's anointing of Saul as king of Israel, or the meeting between Boaz and Ruth. The two characteristics may go together. In other words, in the Old Testament, a miracle implies divine intervention, whether by breaking the rules of creation or arranging for a "fortuitous" event. Yair Zakovich, a professor of biblical studies, defines a miracle as a "divine intervention (overt or concealed) in the rules of creation, either by a break in this order or by means of a 'fortuitous occurrence,' provided that it leaves a strong impression in the literary text."[12] The latter is an important observation, since not every act of divine intervention in the Bible is considered a miracle. Literary criticism of the text of the Old Testament has shown that recognition of an event as a miracle depends on how the event is depicted. Zakovich describes the difference between a perceived miracle and an ordinary action as one between a front page story with photographs and a small news article on an inside page. By analogy, we may say that in oral traditions, as in Africa, such an act should leave a strong impression on the public mind (as miracles do indeed).

The miracles performed by Jesus in the New Testament seem to conform to the same rule as those performed by prophets in the Old Testament. They break the rules of creation (raising Lazarus from the dead) and appear to arrange for a "fortuitous event" (changing water into wine during the wedding at Cana). The difference lies in the believed eschatological meaning of the event in the New Testament, where a connection is made between miracle and proclamation. The miracles performed by Jesus are, for believers, a sign that refers to the coming kingdom of God. The point of reference is Jesus of Nazareth, who, as we may conclude from the New Testament, became widely known as a miracle worker. The gospel stories are full of accounts of the miracles he is said to have performed, although none of these were of a type unique in Jewish history. The Old Testament also contains stories of miraculous healing, raising from the dead, and other miracles performed by prophets. The difference lies in their function. In the Old Testament miracles function not as a sign or symbol—a signifier—but rather as proof or evidence, such as of the power of God. In Africa, it appears, Christian miracles combine effectively the "sign" and the "proof" character of biblical miracles. They are seen as both proof of the power of God and a sign of his kingdom to come. The same can be found in the African diaspora, where church communities often emphasize the miraculous power of God by reference to the second coming of Christ. In that sense, African miracles differ from modern miracles in Europe, whose characteristics display more sign than proof and are more symbol than evidence.

Miraculous events in the defined sense are rather common in Africa. As we have noted, this is partly due to the historical tradition of regular interaction between the visible and the invisible worlds, further influenced by Christian belief in particular. Among the most common miracle stories are apparitions of the Virgin Mary and healing miracles. In recent decades Mary has been claimed, among other episodes, to have appeared to a number of youngsters in Kibeho, in the south of Rwanda; to believers in Cameroon, where she was seen in a tree; in Burkina Faso, where she was said to have appeared in a private house; and in Congo-Brazzaville, where people claimed she had appeared on a wall. Similar apparitions have been reported from Egypt, where she manifested herself in a Coptic church in a popular district of Cairo.

It is not only the Virgin Mary who appears to believers in Africa; sometimes Jesus himself is said to have appeared, even as a person of flesh and blood, anticipating his second coming on earth. According to eyewitness accounts reported in various newspapers, Jesus Christ appeared in Nairobi on 11 June 1988 during a prayer meeting in Kawangware, one of the slums of Nairobi, where a large crowd was addressed by the well-known preacher and healer Mary Akatsa, whom we referred to in Chapter 3. A published photograph showed a tall, slim man, described as swarthy and intense-looking, in white robes and a turban. Believers recognized him as the Son of God. "I am convinced this was a miracle," said Job Mutungi, editor of the Swahili edition of the *Kenya Times*, relating details of the amazing experience. "I saw a bright star in daytime thrice. This person appeared mysteriously in the crowd, and he had a light around his head and sparks from his bare feet." He said that Jesus had blessed the crowd in Swahili, promising them "a bucketful of blessings," after which he left in a car driven by one Mr. Gurnam Singh. On reaching the bus terminus the visitor told Mr. Singh to stop the car as he wanted to alight and head for Heaven. The reporter wrote: "He simply vanished into thin air."[13] These are only some examples of the numerous wondrous stories reported by Christian believers from Africa.

The Domestication of Miracles

Profound religious experiences, whether through dreams, visions, or miracles, serve a purpose, notably that of building faith within a specific religious community. Yet building faith in itself is not enough, as it may not reach beyond the individual level. Institutionally it is important to build the *right type* of faith; hence the need to keep control of the miracle. In Africa, we can see how the domestication of miracles is embedded in the power relations of the Church. With its predominant charismatic character, African Christianity in many cases poses a challenge to established church structures, through its direct accessing of the power of the Holy Spirit. While charismatic believers refuse to restrict the movements of the spirit, the traditional guardians of the faith see to it that certain limits continue to be observed. Control of miracles is one of the instruments of power of a church (or any other religious institution), and a way to keep control over the believers whose words and actions should be guided by the Church. When this happens in western Europe, as it also does, the matter is further complicated by race relations, which have also left their traces in the Church.

Although it is never easy to have some mysterious event recognized as an authentic Christian miracle, it seems almost impossible for an African miracle to conform to the required standards. For a start, the standards are not very clear, and every case is subject to much debate. What *is* clear is that such standards as do exist in the Church have been set in the West. They are highly influenced by Europe's particular history of rational thought, an intellectual tradition that does not easily allow for miraculous events of the type regularly reported from Africa. Determination of standards takes place on the basis of power. The question of who is in control of an alleged miracle is crucial, within a given culture as well as in the relation between different cultures. In practice, this question particularly affects the relations between the Western and the non-Western Church, especially the Catholic Church, given its hierarchical structure. This is also the case because in the Catholic Church miracles have more right to exist than has traditionally been the case in most Protestant churches in the West. Protestant-type churches in Africa that frequently claim miracles are mostly of the African independent or indigenous persuasion, which are free to define their own standards. They may exercise control of a miracle, but this extends only to their own circle.

A good example of the domestication of miracles is probably the most famous of all recent, officially certified miracles in the West, at Medjugorje in former Yugoslavia, where in 1981 the Virgin Mary is believed to have appeared to six village children. After that first appearance the Virgin continued to show herself to the children daily, and Medjugorje became a popular place of pilgrimage. The children continued to receive divine messages through personal visions even after they had reached adulthood. In the course of time, local priests took full control of the process, making sure that the visionaries received their messages at a certain time, at a certain place, and under certain conditions. In other words, the miracle had been domesticated.[14] Steps toward full domestication of the miracle were also taken in Rwanda, where the continuing apparitions of the Virgin Mary incurred strong action on the part of the Catholic Church in a way similar to that in Medjugorje.[15]

In Africa, the domestication of miracles is deemed by the Catholic Church to be even more urgent. The urgency is because, as we noted, they are more frequent, but also because they are more difficult to control by Church authorities due to the geographical and cultural distance between Africa and Europe. For example, it is much easier for the Church to recognize the well-known Italian stigmatist Padre Pio, who is widely considered a saint,[16] than to accept a young Nigerian woman named Pauline Keke in the same category, a woman who every year, on the eve of Easter, starts bleeding profusely from the various spots where Jesus is believed to have bled on the cross. She is not a priest and comes from a culture that is often regarded with some suspicion by the Catholic hierarchy. For Nigerian believers, however, it does not make much difference whether her authenticity as a stigmatist is approved by the Church. People travel from afar to see her bleeding during the last week of Lent, in the hope of sharing in the blessings they believe to be attached to the bleeding phenomenon. In this case, the domestication of the miracle is limited to a few days a year when, particularly on Good Friday, Pauline Keke is admitted to St. Martin's Hospital in Enugu, where she stays during her days of agony.[17]

In recent years we have seen similar efforts toward domestication on the part of the Catholic Church with a view to controlling acclaimed miracles in the field of healing. This has been the case with the healing ministry of Archbishop Milingo, whom the Church removed from Africa to keep him and his work under surveillance in Rome.[18] In fact, the Church has a special department charged with defining the authenticity of an acclaimed miracle. This is considered important because miracles tend to spread their own network of power. A person who is believed able to perform a miracle is considered to be in possession of, or to have access to, a spiritual force that others lack. However, religious experiences in Africa of the sort I have described can never be entirely controlled, since, as I have argued, African religious traditions are essentially charismatic—spirit-oriented. This is particularly evident in the holistic tradition of religious healing on the continent, which takes into account both the physical and spiritual aspects of the human person. This holistic tradition continues in both Christianity and Islam. Many African Christians believe that the manifestations of the Holy Spirit as recorded in the New Testament and experienced in the early Church are still available to them today.

One of the main features in the staging of miracles in Africa is its public character. In Africa, ritual drama of any sort is essentially a community affair, and this also affects the performance of miracles. Official recognition, therefore, is less important than the recognition accorded by the public, which, at the same time, constitutes a further reason for the Church to try and domesticate the miracle.

Miraculous Events and Political Realities

Miracles are just one aspect of a rich field of religious experiences in Africa. Though religiously inspiring for those who experience them, they are of wider interest to those who study African affairs. In a continent where the realms of religion and politics have an impact on one another, their political significance shows itself frequently. We have already noted the political dimension of miraculous events in the case of Kimbangu and Farisani, for example. Since religion and politics are competing realms of power, governments have often tried to suppress spiritual movements. Historical examples include not only the Kimbanguists in the Belgian Congo, but also less well-known spiritual movements such as the one initiated by Zambian prophet Alice Lenshina on the eve of independence.[19] These examples can be complemented with numerous others, past and present, of how believed miraculous happenings have influenced the political course of events. A prominent modern example is the case of Joseph Kony, leader of the Lord's Resistance Army in northern Uganda.

Personal experiences perceived as miracles have such an impact on the public mind that they may influence official politics. In South Africa, there is little doubt about the contribution of religion, institutionalized or based on personal experiences, to fighting the apartheid regime. Similarly, the religious revival that many have observed in Africa in recent years is the result not only of difficult material conditions, but also of creative use of spiritual resources that have proved their effectiveness in the past. This historical tradition has been carried into the diaspora,[20] originally during the time of the slave trade when it gave rise to the so-called black churches. Today, due to international migration, the same tradition has been established all over the world. In Europe we see a similar connection between miraculous belief and political reality in the circumstances of migration. African Christians in Europe frequently apply ideas and theories drawn from the Bible to the often precarious circumstances in which they live. They use them not only to build themselves spiritually but also to criticize what they see as unjust social structures, which lead, for example, to the creation of new borders to exclude foreigners, notably black immigrants. They quote from the Bible to show that God does not recognize frontiers or barriers and that, as children of God, they are as free to move as were the people of Israel. Frontiers are in their view only temporary obstacles to the people of God and will not block their path forever. Sooner or later, God will remove the obstacles erected by man and lead his children into the promised land.

Their contextual reading of the Bible leads African Christians to develop an analysis of what, in their view, are the faults of European society and what should be done to redress them.[21] Typically, their political critique is couched in a spirit idiom, a language not commonly known in the West and therefore rarely understood. In Africa Christian preachers and evangelists circulate popular pamphlets recording their spiritual experiences for the edification of a larger public. By using a spirit idiom they are able to convey their view of politics in Africa in a language easily understood by their listeners.[22]

These observations on the way miraculous experiences relate to politics must be placed in the wider context of the relation between religion and politics in Africa generally. In *Worlds of Power*, Stephen Ellis and I have explored the various ways religious ideas influence political practice in Africa at all levels. We show how religion and politics have been linked throughout African history, a link we see currently revived, including in the dynamics of many new religious movements, Christian and others, that are visibly reoccupying public and political space. African politicians often try to use religious communities to increase their popular base, as politicians do worldwide, including in Europe, where during election campaigns politicians visit places of worship and suddenly demonstrate an active interest in the religious life of migrant communities. The significant difference, however, must be sought at the spiritual level. Whereas in Europe secular politicians might use religion solely as a means of increasing popular support, many African politicians also believe that access to the spiritual world is a vital resource in the constant struggle to secure advantage over their rivals in political infighting. Hence, communication with the spirit world through a variety of techniques we have described in *Worlds of Power* becomes of crucial importance.

Many African heads of state are known to employ religious experts from various traditions in their personal entourage, from born-again pastors to Islamic marabouts and traditional healers or diviners, as well as other religious specialists. This is also done by heads of state not generally regarded as controversial in religious matters, such as Kenneth Kaunda, former president of Zambia, a staunch Christian who nevertheless relied heavily on the services of an Indian guru, Dr. Ranganathan.[23] Like most of their constituents, many African politicians believe that real power has its roots in the invisible world and that therefore the cultivation of spiritual power is vital for their continued political existence.

It remains important to realize that, due to its theological emphasis on the Holy Spirit, African Christianity is generally speaking charismatic in nature, perpetuating the historical tradition of spirit-oriented religions in

Africa. Previously limited to the independent and pentecostal churches in Africa, today it also extends to the historical mainline churches as they undergo a process of charismatization.[24] In my view, this is part of a general "decolonization of the mind" that is taking place in Africa (as in other parts of the world, for that matter) in the post-postcolonial era, whereby the intellectual hegemony of former colonial powers is losing its original weight and significance, both politically and religiously.[25]

Chapter Five
The Problem of Evil:
Religion and Human Rights in Africa

The role of religion—both as an ideology and as a set of institutions channeling ideology—is largely overlooked or ignored in matters of human rights, including in Africa. The protection and promotion of human rights are widely seen as a secular enterprise in which religion has no particular role to play. Inasmuch as religion *is* considered to have a role, it is either as a human rights concern (e.g., concerning the rise of fundamentalism), or as a special source of inspiration for the protection of human rights. In Europe, many human rights activists are practicing Christians. Many of them are known to be members of Amnesty International, for example; its Christian equivalent the Association of Christians Against Torture (ACAT) acts explicitly on the basis of religious inspiration. Many religious bodies, too, are often involved in human rights activities.

This is also the case in Africa. In most countries the Catholic Church is known for its human rights involvement through its Justice and Peace network, while in many conflict-ridden places religious leaders from different faiths are known for their contribution to prevent human rights violations by establishing peace. Recent examples include the Interfaith Council of Liberia and the Acholi Religious Leaders Initiative in northern Uganda, both of which have become known for their mediation to bring an end to hostilities and bring about peace. However, there is rarely a systematic reflection on the potential of religion for the promotion and protection of human rights on the part of secular human rights agents.

Including the religious dimension in the human rights debate is particularly relevant in countries where a majority of people are religious, such as in Africa. Not only are views of human rights often influenced by people's religious beliefs, but such beliefs are also a powerful motive for people to act the way they do. Hence, for an effective human rights policy it is of utmost importance to take religion seriously. This applies not only to religious organizations, but, more important, to the religious *ideas* that are expressed through these bodies and underpin human rights ideas. The discussion on human rights in Africa cannot be detached from African ideas about the nature of evil, which touch on the moral dimension of life. African Christians, as discussed previously, are acutely aware of the existence of evil, manifested often in the form of evil spirits, but also frequently in the form of witchcraft, which is widely considered in Africa as a manifestation of evil stemming from a human source. I will return to this later.

The point at this stage is that certain beliefs about (the nature of) evil have given rise to serious human rights violations in Africa, and continue to do so. Often these are rooted in the specific histories of African countries. Examples include the kinds of horrors committed in recent conflicts, such as those in Liberia, Sierra Leone, and northern Uganda, in which traditional religious beliefs played a significant role.[1] But there are also less conspicuous beliefs and practices that lead to the violation of the rights of women in particular, such as through widowhood rites. Today, the belief in the prevalence of "evil" is frequently commented on by authors studying the latest brand of Christianity in Africa, the charismatic churches, whose preoccupation with deliverance has received much scholarly attention of late. African beliefs about the presence of evil, I argue, have to be taken seriously, even if only for the effect they have on people's lives. In this chapter I will consider this matter from a human rights perspective. To do so it is necessary to consider the relation between religion and human rights in its specific cultural and sociopolitical context, in other words, to localize the issue. But before doing so, I will first discuss the general framework for considering religion in relation to human rights.

Considering Religion in Human Rights

The phrase "human rights" consists of two words. But in human rights discourse the "rights" dimension is often emphasized exclusively, at the expense of the "human" dimension that is integral to the concept. Such an exclusive "rights" approach implies the monopolization of human rights by legal experts, which in my view imposes an unnecessary limitation on the issue. On other occasions I have referred to this as the juridification of human rights. An overwhelmingly juridical approach suggests that all that is needed to ensure respect for the human rights of individuals and groups is to establish a juridical framework that guarantees human rights, for the implementation of which states (or nowadays also others in territorial control) are responsible and can be held accountable. "Rights talk" is important, however, primarily inasmuch as it defines the framework within which a deeper understanding of human rights can be developed. In other words, human rights are not a legal issue only; we also have to consider their moral dimension. The moral-*legal* structure is of obvious importance for the protection of human rights, but in countries marked by a religious outlook on the world it must be matched by a moral-*spiritual* approach to the subject.[2] For many religious believers the moral-spiritual approach to human rights takes priority over the moral-legal one that is characteristic of secular people.

Therefore, we should not limit ourselves in human rights debates to an exclusive focus on the "rights" aspect, but also consider the "human" aspect. We have to ask ourselves not only what it means to have rights, but also what it means to be human.[3] Human rights are claims people are entitled to make simply by virtue of their status as human beings. It begs the question what about a human being makes him or her entitled to make such a claim. To answer that question, the issue of worldview comes into the discussion. For many people in the world, this is a religious, not a secular matter. In Africa, many people believe that a person's spirit links the visible to the invisible or the material to the spiritual world. This spiritual dimension is what makes a person truly human.

In West Africa, for example, we find in various societies, irrespective of the particular type of belief, an idea that a person consists of three different elements that link him or her to the human world, through the maternal and paternal lines of descent respectively, and to the world of spirits, believed to be the place of origin and final destination of humankind. Among the Akan in Ghana or the Yoruba in Nigeria, the spiritual dimension is deemed an essential part of the human condition. If this is so, it means that in considering the rights of human beings, the religious or spiritual aspect cannot be overlooked. It also means that, in societies where the human and spirit worlds are interrelated in a way uncommon in the West, religion may become a dominant factor in establishing human rights, due to a belief that the rights of which human beings dispose have their ultimate origin in the spirit world and are determined by it.[4]

The moral-legal structure of the secular and the moral-spiritual commitment of the religious, however, should be seen not as in opposition but as complementary. Religion and human rights have common ground that can be successfully explored. I would like to submit the following example to illustrate the point. When in 2000 I visited Liberia as part of an Amnesty International mission, during a lull in the civil war that had torn the country apart, I went to Dominion Christian Fellowship Centre, one of the new, large charismatic churches that had sprung up in Monrovia, which congregated in the open air. My presence as a visitor being clearly visible, I was asked at some stage during the service to "take the mike" and address the congregation. For those familiar with this type of church, this is a normal invitation. If, in addition, the invited person is a human rights activist, this is also a golden opportunity to spread the human rights message to a large and willing audience. I had ample time to explain my mission and to speak about human rights, while also addressing the human rights situation in the country. In other words, this provided a unique opportunity for spreading the "secular gospel." After the service, several people, including some junior pastors, came to talk to me, expressing surprise that, as they saw it, we were engaged in similar matters, only from a different perspective. While I was addressing human rights from a secular perspective, they were approaching the same issue from a religious angle.

Similarly, in churches of this type young ex-combatants may give public testimony concerning the often horrific acts they committed during the war. Such testimonies assume the character of a public confession, thereby providing psychological relief; at the same time these young ex-fighters are encouraged by the community of believers, through prayer and fasting, to increase their determination to effect a change of life. Acceptance by the community is of crucial significance to these young men and women, whose antisocial deeds cannot easily be forgotten and forgiven. It is striking how services in these churches are geared toward instilling a sense of self-worth in people whose self-esteem has often been damaged by the experiences they have gone through during the war, which left no one unaffected. In that sense, the charismatic churches are a new type of healing church, building on culturally well-known patterns. The born-again ideology that is so typical of the charismatic churches in Africa is both a reflection and a modern expression of African rites of passage, which have traditionally facilitated individuals in making the transition to a new phase in life with the help of the community. Typically, this is needed when life is at its most vulnerable, at times of crisis, when issues of life and death are at stake.

The Inculturation of Human Rights

The incorporation of the moral-spiritual dimension of human rights would be an important step toward what I call the inculturation of human rights;

that is, such an approach would contribute to the rooting of human rights in local cultures. Religious believers often feel that the way they perceive the world does not find sufficient recognition in the Universal Declaration of Human Rights, which they tend to see largely as the product of secular developments. It is therefore important to recognize, as former Czech president and human rights activist Václav Havel has also argued, the spiritual dimension and origin of the values guarded by the United Nations, and to translate this into the organization's practical activities.

The values underlying the Universal Declaration are indeed truly universal, but they are expressed differently in different cultures. One of the weaknesses of much current human rights discourse is the lack of appreciation for the specific contribution of local cultures to the universal concept of human rights. We have to make clear, therefore, that universalizing human rights is not the same as Westernizing them. The inculturation of human rights must be a *two-way* process, in which Western proponents of human rights learn and accept that certain values derived from a culture that is originally not theirs may actually be of use to them, too. For a successful inculturation of human rights in all parts of the world, we have to give serious thought to the role played by religion as an integral part of people's existence, inseparable from the social and moral order. For religion is not only about relations between human and spirit beings. It also defines people's relations with their fellow human beings, which is central to the concept of human rights.

If this is the case, it becomes very important to engage ourselves much more than is normally the case with religious *ideas* at a grassroots level, and to see how we can do so for the sake of human rights. Inasmuch as human rights debates involve religious actors at all, they mostly engage religious elites, that is, the leaders of religious organizations and not the mass of believers, whose views are often far less sophisticated and less informed than those of their leaders. This is also the case in Africa. We often know very little about what ordinary people believe in matters of human rights, as their views are usually mediated by others: politicians and religious and other leaders.

Some years ago I initiated a small research network with colleagues in Africa to investigate concepts of human rights in a bottom-up approach. The project sought to explore human rights ideas among ordinary religious believers, notably in African-initiated churches, of both the classical type ("spiritual" churches) and the new type (charismatic churches). This required, first and foremost, empirical research among ordinary churchgoers to find out what they think, rather than a theological research approach based on normative and prescriptive ideas. What sorts of ideas do these church members hold with regard to what we call human rights? What types of rights do they ascribe to human beings? It is important to understand the mentality of people if we want to influence their thought. In the Western world human rights work in Africa is often connected with the former mission churches, at both the theoretical and the practical level. This is due partly to the specific historical conditions under which human rights activities have developed in Africa, but also to a widespread supposition that African-initiated churches have no interest in such matters because of their spiritual focus. Many church communities, however, are often dealing with questions of human rights without labeling them as such.

Our research was based on the assumption that in many countries people at the grassroots level have no clear conception of human rights as formulated in the Universal Declaration of Human Rights. They may not even know the term, since they may be illiterate. They do know, however, when life treats them well and when it does not, and they can tell what is beneficial and what is harmful to them. Therefore the questions that guided our research had to be formulated in such a way as to allow individual believers to phrase in their own way whatever ideas or views they might have that are relevant to the subject. In short, there is no point in asking such people what they think about "human rights." A more circumstantial and nuanced way has to be used to investigate popular views on human rights in African-initiated churches. We have been trying to find answers to questions such as:

- What understanding do members of these churches have of what it means to be "human"?
- What kind of ideas do they associate with this concept?
- Are there any sorts of people who are not considered fully human, and if so: why?
- What values do they cherish in this respect?
- What do they consider important in their lives and for what reasons?
- What aspects of life do they consider vital for a "good" life?
- How do they think they can achieve and promote a good life?
- How does this relate to a good life for others?
- What sort of factors may, or do, hamper a good life, both for oneself and for others?
- What sort of ideas do they have about "evil" and what constitutes evil in their view?
- How do they relate this to their ideas of humanity?

Research of this type is also important in that we often see that people who are guilty of gross human rights violations have, prior to their act, dehumanized the victim. That is, they have decided that their opponent is not a "real" human being and therefore is not entitled to human rights and may be treated differently from "real" human beings. In Africa, a notorious example is the 1994 genocide in Rwanda, where organs of state and mass communication consistently conveyed the message that part of the population were actually "cockroaches" and therefore should be eliminated. This discourse appeared persuasive to at least some Christian believers, including individual priests and nuns.[5]

By stating matters this way, I am not suggesting that we should respect whatever ideas people, in whatever part of the world, including the Western world, may hold in this regard. There cannot be any cultural exceptions to what is regarded as "human" or "humane" by the international community on the basis of the Universal Declaration of Human Rights. But to reach universal consensus, it is of the greatest importance first to know what people believe, for what reasons, and to what effect. We should not deny legitimacy to the right of different societies to develop their own methods for solving problems of human rights within the framework of the Declaration. In fact, sensitivity to cultural diversity is, in my view, a precondition for the successful inculturation of human rights. Cultural sensitivity—open-mindedness about the potentials of unfamiliar cultures—is not the same as cultural relativism. Whereas cultural sensitivity makes possible a process of dialogue that can be mutually enriching, cultural relativism leads to a separate development of human rights.

This argument implies that we cannot and should not accept everything related to traditional culture as a legitimate expression of local values, whether in Europe or in Africa. In the latter case, there are a number of widespread practices, often based on a traditional religious worldview, that are highly problematic from a human rights perspective and therefore deserve attention from all those engaged in human rights locally. Consider the custom of female ritual servitude widespread in certain parts of Africa, which has led to serious forms of abuse in modern times; forms of trial by ordeal that may include administering poison or burning skin; accusations of witchcraft that often lead to killing alleged witches; the disturbing rate of what are commonly referred to as "ritual killings"; the discriminatory and often humiliating practices related to widowhood rites in many parts of the continent. These are only some examples. One of the disturbing aspects is the gender bias in these types of human rights abuse, as they mostly affect women and girls. From women's point of view, "culture" is being used as an excuse for outdated discriminatory practices, often validated by the numerous taboos affecting women and womanhood. A study carried out by the Catholic Church in the northern region of Ghana uncovered a range of taboos that prevent women from gaining access to positions of economic independence. For example, they are not allowed to farm cash crops, possess a hoe, have livestock, and so on. Widowhood rites are another example. These are rites that must be performed to appease the spirit of the deceased, and as such are another expression of the need to ward off evil. They are physically and psychologically demanding and, though once accepted as normal, are today considered degrading for women.

In the following, I limit the discussion to one widespread phenomenon in Africa, witchcraft, which is based on traditional religious beliefs but has not disappeared, as may have been expected, under the influence of Christianity. In fact, the Church has generally failed to address the issue in an effective manner, largely because it refuses to acknowledge the essential spiritual nature of witchcraft for many Africans.

Witchcraft Accusations as a Human Rights Concern

The term "witchcraft" refers to a widespread belief that certain people possess the power to cause harm by mystical means. The belief in witchcraft as a mystical force used to harm others is essentially a religious idea. It is part of a much broader complex of ideas concerning an invisible world, believed to be the abode of spiritual beings and other spirit forces with which people communicate and interact. People accused of practicing witchcraft run into deep trouble, as they are liable to be severely punished for their alleged antisocial behavior. They may be maltreated, chased from their village or otherwise banned from the community, and even killed. Evidence from a large number of African countries indicates that witchcraft accusations are rampant and, in recent years, have led to the unlawful killing, exiling, or imprisonment of many individuals. Even more recently, witchcraft accusations against children have been recorded from various places, including African religious communities in Britain[6] and elsewhere in Europe.

Witchcraft beliefs amount to a moral theory that, as history has shown in Africa, can neither be legislated out of existence nor eliminated through formal education. The anti-witchcraft legislation introduced in African countries under colonial rule brought no real solution to witchcraft-related problems. In general, such laws forbid both witchcraft accusations and the practice of techniques likely to be considered witchcraft-related. Colonial governments did not take any position on the reality of witchcraft, but tried only to suppress witchcraft accusations in an attempt to make African societies conform to European ideas of right and wrong. In practice, this meant that colonial magistrates often ended up condemning the accusers rather than the perceived manipulators of evil, or "witches," in any specific incident. As a result, African communities felt abandoned to the capricious powers of witches, against whom they had no legal defense. Whatever defensive measures they took would done outside the formal jurisdiction of colonial law.

Colonial law did not succeed in suppressing witchcraft practices and accusations. Witchcraft accusations have remained part of life in many African communities. At the heart of this failure lies the fact that the law is unable to address the moral-spiritual dimension of the matter, which accompanies the moral-legal dimension upheld by the law. One result of this imbalance is a frequent lack of commitment to upholding the law on the part of law enforcement officers, either because they themselves believe an accused person is a witch or because they are afraid being accused of witchcraft if they are seen to protect a witch, someone considered an enemy of society. Many Africans see witchcraft as a very dangerous form of evil, and they may act accordingly.

According to Peter Sarpong, one of the Catholic bishops of Ghana, who has written about the subject, the effect of the belief in witchcraft on people's social life is tremendous. For example, he says, the belief that somebody can give you a gift that contains witchcraft substance makes parents warn their children not to receive gifts from old people especially. When people are sick, they will not stay near their home because it is believed that witches strike at short range. If you are far from home, they cannot strike you. So a person going to have a medical operation may either not tell anybody in his or her immediate circle for fear that witches may make use of the occasion to attack them, or travel far away to have the operation.[7] That the witches' range-limits may not be considered effective any more, I learned during my own work among Ghanaian migrant communities in the Netherlands, where people believe that "witches" now also travel overseas to strike their victim.[8] In Ghana, it is mostly believed that the person who can bewitch you is most likely to be a close relative. Witchcraft power is thought to reside in a fiery substance that is inside a person and gets out of her (most of the time) during the night to join others with similar powers. Among the Akan of Ghana, witches, or witchcraft spirits, are believed to stay on the tops of trees. During my various travels there I heard several stories to that effect from people who claimed to have been eyewitnesses. Witches are also believed to feed on human flesh, and have to take their turns in supplying it.[9] This explains why a person's sudden death or gradual waning away may easily be blamed on somebody else.

It is worth noting in this context that, although witchcraft and evil spirits are both perceived as manifestations of evil, they are not one and the same thing. While evil spirits are believed to be external forces that enter a person involuntarily and take up temporary residence, witchcraft powers are a type of evil that is inherent, voluntary, and permanent. This difference in character makes it far more difficult for a religious specialist, whether traditional or Christian, to free people from witchcraft powers than from evil spirits. Witchcraft beliefs are particularly harmful when social relations are disrupted and these beliefs give rise to some form of action. When that happens, witchcraft accusations will be publicly voiced, often setting in motion a series of events that eventually lead to the death of the accused. Figure 1 provides a graphic image of the dangerous escalation process that may take place if witchcraft accusations are not controlled.[10]

The model shows that people may respond rather differently to witchcraft accusations. Some societies do not adhere to notions of witchcraft and deal with tension in a different way. Those who believe that witchcraft exists appear to have a range of options: they may recognize the problems believed to emerge from it but desist from taking action, they may express suspicions and pursue them, they may accuse specific people of using witchcraft, they may actually formulate witchcraft accusations, and they may eventually kill alleged witches, whether by due process of law or—more often—lynching or mob justice. But at each step those who fear that witchcraft may be involved have the option of halting the escalation.

Witchcraft beliefs, then, are widespread in Africa, as can be seen in the figure. Such beliefs often lead to forms of social action that affect the human rights of individual people, in varying degrees depending on the degree to which the ensuing social conflict escalates. In South Africa, people accused of witchcraft may end up in what are popularly known as "witch villages" to avoid being lynched. Basically, these are places of rescue where alleged witches, mostly women, may find at least some degree of security and protection. In Ghana, too, there are special places, known as "witch camps," where individuals accused of witchcraft, almost exclusively women, have sought refuge and escaped from certain death. "Witch villages" and "witch camps" are rather unfortunate expressions for places of refuge, miserable though they may be, for people accused of witchcraft who have been chased away from their village or escaped being lynched.

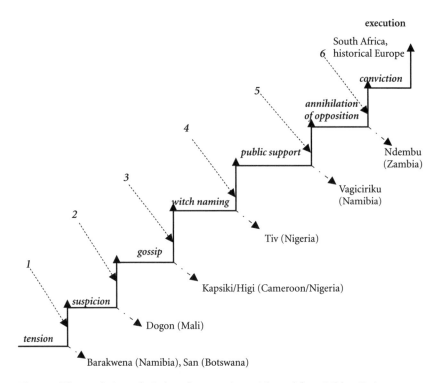

Figure 1. The escalation of witchcraft accusations. Adapted from Walter E. A. van Beek, "The Escalation of Witchcraft Escalations," in Gerrie ter Haar, ed., *Imagining Evil: Witchcraft Beliefs and Accusations in Contemporary Africa* (Trenton, N.J.: Africa World Press, 2007), 308.

In South Africa alleged witches have often been burned to death; in Ghana lynchings often mean being stoned to death. Yet there are differences in the conditions surrounding the issue, mainly due to the particular stance of government officials and nongovernmental organizations. One striking and important difference is the attitude toward the law. In South Africa, there is a strong faction lobbying for a change of law permitting legal prosecution of alleged witches, on the grounds that witchcraft is "real" and therefore practicing it should be considered a crime, irrespective of Western public opinion and international human rights stipulations. This is a point of view shared by several other African countries. If such a change in the law is implemented, victims of witchcraft accusations will be prosecuted. In Ghana, however, it is the accused, not the accuser, who is protected by law. Although Ghanaian authorities are facing similar problems in trying to suppress witchcraft accusations, the law is applied not to prosecute but to protect victims of witchcraft accusations.

Nongovernmental organizations have also engaged with the issue. In Ghana, the Presbyterian Church in particular has considered the plight of the mostly old women living in so-called witch camps. In the village of Gambaga in northern Ghana, it was originally the chief imam who, over a century ago, out of sympathy offered to receive and take care of the women. But as the number of women seeking refuge increased over time, successive imams appealed to the local chief for land for settlement and asked for material support for the women. The present chief of Gambaga, himself a traditional ruler and believer in witchcraft powers, has responded to the request in a traditional religious way. He pours libation to invoke the spirits of the ancestors to assist in rendering the women's alleged powers harmless. Subsequently, the women have to go through certain rituals before they are allowed to settle on his land. It is relevant in this context to know that the chief is believed to possess a spiritual antidote against witchcraft powers, which is applied after a rite in which the guilt or innocence of the accused is confirmed. So, what we see is that, although a safe haven has been created in this way for the accused women, nevertheless in many cases they are still believed to be "witches."[11]

In fact, such places of refuge have been in existence for decades in Ghana, but it was only in 1997 that, because of a media report, "witch camps" became a national issue. Several organizations, including the government Commission on Human Rights and Administrative Justice, investigated the situation and inspected living conditions, notably in Gambaga. According to the chief, their relatives brought most of the women to him, some at the point of death, others having received severe beatings from people in their communities. When I visited him in 2001, he explained that the women are allowed to return home if they wish, but they refuse for fear of being killed. Normally, the communities do not want the women back, and cases have been reported where women have been killed on return. It is here that the Presbyterian Church has stepped in with a project known as the "Go Home Project," which aims at returning the accused women to their families and communities. The main goals of the project are to educate families and communities to desist from sending alleged witches to what is in fact an outcast home and to assist in the rehabilitation of returnees, to help the women in Gambaga to earn their own income, and to improve their health. Although it is a long and slow process, this church project has certainly achieved some of its goals, as living conditions in Gambaga have considerably improved and acceptance of the women as part of the larger village has increased, as has the number of returnees.

Sometimes, when a community refuses to take a particular woman back, the church seeks resettlement and reintegration elsewhere.[12]

Religion as a Source of Human Rights

The perceived spiritual nature of evil among African believers often prevents Western-based and -trained institutions or individuals from making common cause with them in their fight for human rights and against human rights abuses. In fact, witchcraft accusations are rarely considered in human rights terms at all, but seen as a culture-specific expression of social tensions. The situation is similar for many other traditional religious beliefs that have received little to no attention from a human rights perspective and have not engaged the Christian Church.

One of these concerns *trokosi*, a practice in West Africa by which young girls—virgins—are attached to a local shrine in retribution for crimes or "sins" committed by other members of the family, usually men. These girls become the slaves, often sex slaves, of the traditional priests serving at the shrines. This practice, believed to have its origins in Benin, has been publicly exposed only since the early 1990s. At that time, a Ghanaian Christian NGO mediated on behalf of the government to negotiate the freedom of these girls. Subsequently 92 were released at just one major shrine. By the year 2000, some 2,000 girls and women were said to have been set free, while another 2,000 were still held at various shrines in southeast Ghana. This form of female ritual servitude, as we may call the phenomenon, is also reflected in the current practice of human trafficking from Africa to Europe. Young Nigerian girls who have fallen victim to human traffickers are ritually bonded to a local shrine. The bondage has been established by the traditional priest by catching the girl's soul for the sake of the human trafficker, who can now use her as a sex slave in the West. She is forced into prostitution, and is manipulated through the fear that she or other members of her family will die if she breaks the oath by disobedience or escape. Part of the tragedy is that in Europe only a few people seem prepared to believe these stories, and even fewer understand the meaning of them. Since the religious dimension is frequently dismissed, care for these young prostitutes is usually left to interested churches. It is ironic, perhaps, that in the Netherlands, for example, a prestigious award was given to Ghanaian pastor Tom Marfo, who has made it his business to "save" these girls by addressing the issue as both a social and a religious problem.

Clearly, there is an urgent need for human rights activists and others to engage in a constructive dialogue with "local custom," not with a view to legitimizing existing practices that may be considered to violate the human rights of women, but to make pragmatic use of the dynamics of culture to help realize gender equality. In order to do this, the spiritual nature of evil, as people believe and experience it, must be addressed. Any acceptable human rights framework should be able to mediate in the inevitable conflict between human rights and cultural norms and practices, which often contain a religious dimension. It has often been argued by African intellectuals, including theologians, that traditional African societies have always at least implicitly acknowledged the concept of human rights, at both an individual and communal level. This in itself provides evidence of Africa's potential to create a new framework for defining the human rights dimension of the relationship between the individual, the community, and the state. Part of that potential lies in the possibility consciously to mobilize religion as a source for human rights. Bringing in the religious dimension implies looking seriously at people's notions of evil, which have been shaped by the historical and cultural traditions in which Africans stand. Without doing so, secular attempts to prevent human rights violations may have only a temporary effect.

The question of mobilizing spiritual resources for the "common good" is not limited to the issue of human rights. In the next chapter I will make a case for including religion—in its various modes of expression—in the development debate.

Chapter Six

Abundant Life in Africa: Religion and Development

The relevance and rationale of religion in the development debate, with specific reference to sub-Saharan Africa, poses the same question we raised when discussing human rights, albeit in a different context: namely, how can Africa's religious resources can be mobilized for development? Africa is generally considered to be the poorest continent of all, a view which is supported by figures and other economic data provided by international financial institutions such as the World Bank and the International Monetary Fund (IMF). Its poor economic conditions are often aggravated by lack of "good governance," failing states, or conflict situations, as well as the AIDS pandemic, which has hit the continent hard and is wiping out the economically most productive age group of the population. Together, these developments have strengthened the essential idea in the West that Africa is a continent to be helped. So it was in the past, and so it is now.

The external ambition to "improve" Africa goes back to eighteenth-century Europe. It first emerged among evangelical Christians, the main initiators of the anti-slavery movement. In the nineteenth century, the European missionary movement inspired programs of education and health services as part of a larger aspiration to "civilize" Africa. The idea of development thus has antecedents that go back for over two centuries. However, the specific notion of developing Africa on the basis of scientifically validated principles, implemented by technocrats in a secular mode, essentially emerged in the years after the end of World War II in 1945. From the start, modern ideas about development generally overlooked the role of religion in Africa, or assumed that it would be relegated to a matter of private belief as secular states gained strength and confidence, or even represented religion as an obstacle to development. Yet it is now apparent that religion is a growing force in public life in Africa, as in many other parts of the world.

Clearly, this phenomenon has implications for the development process. The role of religion in development, including in Africa, is currently a subject of intense debate among both governmental and nongovernmental development agents, some of whom are beginning to acknowledge and address the need for new paradigms in development thought. This awareness relates to other attempts, outside the immediate sphere of religion, to mobilize people's spiritual resources for development, encompassing the full range of human life. Concepts such as "spiritual capital," "spiritual empowerment," and "spiritual investment" have been introduced by a variety of thinkers and actors to broaden the debate to include that elusive dimension, which to many Africans, as well as others in the non-Western world, constitutes a real presence and power.

In their book *Spiritual Capital: Wealth We Can Live By*, Danah Zohar and Ian Marshall identify spiritual intelligence (SQ) as a particular form of intelligence, different from rational intelligence (IQ) and emotional intelligence (EQ). They argue that spiritual capital forms the underlying base for any other kind of capital, including material capital. Spiritual intelligence, in their view, is what provides a sense of meaning and values and of fundamental purpose on which to build spiritual capital, that is, the wealth that these can generate. They argue that "It is only when our notion of capitalism includes spiritual capital's wealth that we can have sustainable capitalism and a sustainable society."[1] People, organizations, and cultures that have spiritual capital, they maintain, will be more sustainable because they will have developed a broader range of qualities, notably addressing concerns about what it means to be human. This, we saw in the previous chapter, is one of the questions most urgently needing to be addressed in the human rights debate. It has also been addressed in recent years by United Nations agencies, whose annual worldwide Human Development Reports have appeared since 1990. The title indicates that development is more than a technical process that can be approached by conventional means only. All this throws a different light on the potential role of religion in the development process.

Exploring Religious Resources for Development

Until recently, the religious dimension of the lives of individuals and communities has been largely ignored in development cooperation, or even dismissed as irrelevant or harmful. This neglect may well have had a negative effect on development cooperation. As some observers have pointed out,[2] many of the major flaws in the development process have arisen from a failure to come to grips with the metaphysical questions concerning human life that provide the framework for any meaningful debate about the aims of development and how to understand and measure progress or the nature of the "good life." In African terms, we may—following Tanzanian theologian Laurenti Magesa—talk about an abundant life, which, typically, is enjoyed in community with other beings, not only human but also spirit ones.[3] In Africa, both philosophers and theologians have argued, the concept of prosperity cannot be reduced to its economic aspect but encompasses the spiritual dimension. As in so many other countries in the non-Western world, religion is part of the social fabric and fully integrated with other dimensions of life. This is a simple social fact, but with important consequences for development cooperation.

In Africa, I have argued in previous chapters, the invisible world is an integral part of the world as people know it; the world is not reduced to its visible or material form only, and people's social relations extend into the invisible world. That is, in the same way they try to maintain good relations with their relatives, neighbors, and friends, individuals and communities invest in their relations with spiritual entities to enhance the quality of life. They enter into active communication with the spirit world and derive information from it to further their material welfare or interests. Spirit-oriented religious traditions create their own dynamics that may be employed for development purposes. One obvious example is the great variety of healing traditions using methods based on an intimate knowledge of, and regular contact with, the spirit world. I have referred to this earlier as "spiritual technology" (see Chapter 1). Accessing such power is generally considered important, especially when people have no recourse to other sources of power. Through communication with an invisible or spirit world people can share in a form of power that can transform their lives. As we saw earlier, in societies with a historical tradition of active engagement with a spirit world, great esteem is accorded to those who are able to delegate control voluntarily to a spiritual power for as long as needed.

The Concept of Development

Let us first take a closer look at the concept of development. The modern idea of development has a genealogy in Western Christianity and can be seen as the secular translation of a millenarian belief whereby the kingdom of God is no longer projected in heaven but can be created on earth. Inherent in this thinking is the aspiration to eliminate evil in all its forms from the earth and the belief that human beings will eventually achieve this goal. This ideology stands in rather sharp contrast to a religious worldview that recognizes human imperfection and generally accepts that life will never be perfect. The real challenge in life is then to balance the powers of good and evil in such a way that evil will not prevail.

The belief in progress so characteristic of modern development theory also reflects the Christian idea of humankind as pilgrims on the road to their final destination, where life will be as originally intended by its creator. In modern times, this religious notion of progress has become secularized and largely applied to material progress. Hence, development cooperation often pays too little attention to the road to development, which for religious believers is often at least as important as the goal. While a secular worldview places its main emphasis on goals and objectives, a religious worldview tends to emphasize the ways to achieve them. But there are some other significant differences between secular and religious approaches in development cooperation. While a secular approach stresses the role of the individual, a religious approach is more likely to emphasize the importance of the community. Other significant contrasts concern a mechanistic versus an organic view of society, a competition versus cooperation model, and the importance attached to the output of economic activities versus the input required.[4] In western Europe in particular, the secularization of society has caused many people to overlook the original connection between religion and the notion of development. People who are religious, however, are more likely to make this connection.

Religiously inspired views of development, then, are not primarily concerned with questions of economic development. One commentator observed already a quarter of a century ago that development experts seem to religious believers to be "one-eyed giants," who "analyse, prescribe and act *as if* man could live by bread alone, *as if* human destiny could be stripped to its material dimensions alone."[5] For many religious people the spiritual dimension precedes the material one, in the sense that prosperity cannot be achieved without creating the spiritual conditions conducive to that goal. Hence, they consider inner transformation a necessary condition for social transformation, or even an actual source of it. Charismatic Christians, for example, of whom there are many in Africa, generally believe that to improve a country's condition one has first to work at changing the hearts and minds of its leaders. From a religious perspective, without spiritual progress there can be no sustainable material progress.

The question whether religion can make a contribution to development has been discussed for some years now in various circles. Recent research suggests that there is a clear need to give more space to the religious or spiritual dimension of human existence in development thought, as a counterbalance to the neoliberal, free-market policies whose consequences are acutely felt by the developing countries on which structural adjustment programs (SAPs) were imposed by the World Bank and the IMF.[6] This awareness has also entered these very financial institutions. Since 1994, the World Bank, at that time still under the leadership of James Wolfensohn, has taken an interest in religion, motivated by the growing number of NGOs that criticized the Bank at its fiftieth anniversary for what they considered its "destructive, undemocratic and unaccountable policies."[7] In 1995, a joint World Bank-NGO committee was created to review structural adjustment programs. In the name of "good governance," the World Bank has come to recognize and encourage a role for religion, ethics, and spirituality.[8] Since 1994, it has sponsored several international conferences on religion and religion-related issues, in close cooperation with representatives of various religious traditions. At one such occasion, the 1995 Conference on Ethics and Spiritual Values, Bank president Wolfensohn publicly stated that the Bank's central mission is "to meld economic assistance with spiritual, ethical and moral development."[9] In 1998 he co-hosted a conference on World Faiths and Development with archbishop of Canterbury George Carey, known to be of evangelical persuasion, representing a trend in Christianity particularly popular in the southern hemisphere. In a concluding joint statement it was agreed, among other things, that human development must have regard for spiritual, ethical, environmental, cultural, and social considerations; that religious communities would be allowed to influence World Bank thinking and had in fact already contributed much to development projects; and that governments and international agencies would be exhorted to join the search for a better understanding between religion and development.[10]

The approach taken by the World Bank at the time resonates with the view of the United Nations Development Programme (UNDP), which has stated that human development "is about creating an environment in which people can develop their full potential and lead productive, creative lives in accord with their needs and interests."[11] It thus refers to people's resources beyond any purely material aspect.

Religion and Development in Africa

Introducing religion into the development debate is not uncontroversial. The question has been explicitly raised how a spiritual vision can help solve the complex issues of our day.[12] The role of, and contribution to, development played by religious institutions and religious leaders has been recorded in many places and situations, past and present, notably in the fields of education and public health. By and large, this is a much appreciated role, which in Africa is mostly connected with the former mission churches. Far less is known, however, about the religious ideas that underlie religious communities' actual behavior, a point we noted with regard to the human rights debate. There is an urgent need here, too, to understand other people's worldviews, as sustained development needs to be based on the cosmology of the people concerned.

An instructive example comes from Zimbabwe, one of the last countries in Africa to gain independence, in 1980. During the *chimurenga*, as the liberation war is known, spirit mediums conveyed directives from the spirit world to commanders and fighters, influencing the tactics of the war. In this case, the guiding spirits were royal ancestor spirits (*mhondoro*), considered the "guardians of the land." They were believed to be united in a spirit war council presided over by Mwari, the most important deity of the Shona (the largest population group in Zimbabwe), where they made decisions about the course of the liberation war. After the war, the role of spirit mediums in inspiring the guerrilla fighters and mobilizing peasant support in Zimbabwe became widely known, notably through the publication of a highly successful book by David Lan.[13]

After independence many Zimbabweans came to realize that they might have politically reconquered the land, but that ecologically this had not at all been the case. Africa's woodlands have generally been vanishing fast, for a great variety of reasons: population growth, an ever-increasing need for firewood, the lucrative timber trade, the need to clear land to plant cash crops, and so on. In Zimbabwe, some 3–4 percent of the total land surface is said to be deforested every year. As a result, there is soil erosion, desertification, and general degradation of the land. This disastrous situation led in the late 1980s to a unique initiative in southern Zimbabwe to reverse the process, in collaboration with local communities. For that purpose, communities once again sought the help of the spirit mediums, who this time embarked on "the war of the trees."[14] Liberation of the "lost lands" had to take the form of massive mobilization of peasant communities to join in tree planting, wildlife conservation, and protection of water resources. This awareness led to the establishment of three interrelated institutions to guide activities in the rural areas of Masvingo province: an umbrella organization called the Zimbabwean Institute of Religious Research and Ecological Conservation (ZIRRCON) and its two affiliates the Association of Zimbabwean Traditional Ecologists (AZTREC) and the Association of African Earthkeeping Churches (AAEC). Together they initiated new ecological conservation programs through local community participation, in which traditional believers and members of African independent churches worked hand in hand with local scientists.

This interesting combination of organizations shows how academic and religious initiatives can work together effectively in development matters. While ZIRRCON notably consisted of trained researchers, AZTREC consisted mainly of spirit mediums, chiefs, and former guerrilla fighters who had redefined the liberation struggle. They were calling on the spirit world where the ancestors reside, the "guardians of the land," this time to receive instructions about how to fight the "war of the trees." The third organization, AAEC, consisted of a large number of so-called African independent churches, also known as "prophetic" or "healing churches." They based themselves on Christian principles, deriving their inspiration and power from their belief in the Holy Spirit. They interpreted the war of the trees as the movement of the earth-keeping Spirit that seeks to "clothe" the land with life-restoring vegetation. A new theology of the environment was being developed.

Ecology is only one important area of development. Another is poverty reduction, the primary goal of most development organizations, national and international, as the UN Millennium Development Goals (MDGs) testify. The first of the eight MDGs states as its aspiration a halving of extreme poverty and hunger by the year 2015. However, in this case, too, it is interesting to see that for those concerned in the developing world poverty is not a material issue only. When Ghana was officially labeled a heavily indebted and poor (HIPC) country, this was resented by some Ghanaians, who rejected the label on the grounds that they might not be materially very wealthy, but they were in possession of a rich spiritual culture. From their own perspective, they were not poor at all, and they felt insulted by the imposition of an identity that insulted their sense of pride, creating an image that found no resonance in Ghanaians' self-image, ignoring the fact that development begins with people's self-understanding.

Another area where the religious dimension proves of crucial importance is the health sector. For many people in the world healing is a holistic activity, in conformity with a worldview that does not separate the spiritual and material dimensions of life. In Africa, as we have noted, illness is generally seen in terms of everything that hinders human well-being and prevents people from developing their human potential, materially or spiritually. Hence, it seems important for development organizations to respond to people's needs by integrating spiritual ideas into health care policies. (A similar need has been identified among migrant communities in the West.) This is particularly urgent in view of the HIV/AIDS pandemic in Africa. It is ironic, to say the least, that many Africans not only think that AIDS is somehow spread from the West, but also make a connection between the words "AIDS" and "aid," which also comes from the most developed countries.[15] This is not simply a linguistic mistake that can be explained with reference to an oral culture, but reflects a profound ambiguity in the ideas people in Africa have about the nature of power emanating from the West. Moreover, the purely technical approach of Western development organizations that propagate the use of condoms as the main means to prevent AIDS negates the need to address the issue at the spiritual level, too, considering, among other things, the need for numerous offspring to reach ancestor status and more generally people's ideas about abundant life, of which fertility is an important aspect. It is all related to what Laurenti Magesa refers to as the "mystique of life"[16] as perceived by many Africans.

The Prosperity Gospel

In recent years, the concept "prosperity gospel" has been introduced in the literature, particularly with regard to the latest and fastest growing brand of Christian churches in Africa, the charismatic churches. There is a vast literature on the subject, mostly by Western scholars and commentators who implicitly or explicitly disapprove of the phenomenon. They have commonly observed that the so-called prosperity gospel hampers Africa's economic development by "spiritualizing" politics (an argument, it is worth noting, that had previously been used in the debate on classical African-initiated churches), which distracts Africans from devoting themselves to more urgent business.[17] Such commentators, in my view, show a lack of insight into some important implications of a religious or spiritual approach to development. Like so many conventional development agents, rather than seeing human development as a *process*, they see it in terms of practical results to be achieved in a set period of time. Such observers will also not connect, for example, the popular concern with demonic evil with questions of morality, as Africans themselves might do. In the critics' view, a preoccupation with evil only diverts attention from more important practical matters. Similarly, they will not even consider the possibility that "implicit politics" can have a positive effect on the political situation in Africa. Most important, many observers continue to analyze events in Africa in terms primarily derived from a mindset and intellectual framework shaped by the historical conditions of the West, notably western Europe. They are unwilling or unable to rework their mental framework so as to incorporate what Andrew Walls has called the "open frontier" nature of African worldviews,[18] where, as I have argued throughout this book, interaction between the material and the spiritual world is both common and normal.

The idea that the religious dimension is crucial for material development is not unique to Africa. Historically, in Europe material prosperity used to be seen as a sign of virtue and divine blessing. It is widely acknowledged that religious ideas played an important part in the development of capitalism in Europe. This was not primarily as a result of direct action by religious institutions, but through the influence of religious ideas on people's thinking concerning the legitimacy of wealth and the moral value of certain financial operations, such as lending, saving, or investing money. Thus the significance of religious ideas in forming people's ideas about material prosperity expresses itself differently at various times and places.

Ghanaian theologian Kingsley Larbi has pointed out that prosperity refers to "the ability to live a happy and balanced life without the problem of having to think what to eat, where to sleep, what to wear; how to meet one's social expectations, like school fees, children's education and the ability to contribute to the need of one's community."[19] The religious message, he argues, must be placed within the social and economic realities of a country, and understood in terms of traditional concepts of life, for it to be appreciated. There is an undeniable relation between the visible and invisible worlds in the sense that a person who is in good spiritual health can also expect to prosper materially. The so-called prosperity gospel promises access to "power which will cater for the necessities of life and protect it from its vicissitudes— a life that is full, prosperous, healthy, peaceful and secure."[20] These are all concerns that address basic human needs in the opinion of Western development agents as well.

Spiritual health as a necessary condition for material wealth is precisely the condition African-initiated churches in Europe aspire to bring about in their members when they try to promote the "good life" through the power of the Holy Spirit. In order to prosper, they equally believe, one must depend on God. This appears to be as true for African traditional believers as for Christian adherents, whether in Africa or Europe. It is interesting, in this regard, that African charismatic churches that are operating worldwide, as we will see in the following chapter, have set up their own ministries through which they also pursue development goals. The difference from conventional development agents is that they have made spirituality the heart of their endeavors. Hence, provision of spiritual support is key to their efforts to improve the quality of life of their members. For example, the Redeemed Christian Church of God (RCCG), one of the largest African-initiated charismatic churches in Africa, with headquarters in Nigeria, runs an AIDS program known as RAPAC, the Redeemed AIDS Programme Action Committee, based on spiritual principles.[21] It receives part of its money from USAID/Nigeria. Clearly African religious initiatives are increasingly operating on their own terms, determined in the first instance by Africans' spiritual needs, which, as we have seen, also affect their material lives.

Milingo and Development

The unique focus of Western observers on what they consider "spiritualizing" politics easily leads them to ignore the intellectual contribution made by Africans to theories of development. A prime example is Zambian archbishop Emmanuel Milingo, who among Western observers is best known for his ability to exorcize demons, and whose writings on development, dating to the early 1970s and continuing to the present, have been entirely ignored. His thinking about development shows the holistic approach which is so evident in African religious worldviews generally and which refuses to equate human development with the material progress of a nation. Milingo's understanding of development refers to "the freeing of human potentialities to be channelled to the profitable use for the individual himself as well as for the community in which he is living."[22] This process, he wrote more than thirty years ago, must lead individuals to a change of attitude toward life, and help them realize what they have (their potentialities), and what they can do for themselves (building self-confidence). Development, thus, should aim at educating people to be aware of what they are and what they can do.

   Over the years Archbishop Milingo has been highly critical of the development theories of Western agencies and aid workers, who, in his view, have not really taken into consideration the role of ordinary men and women in the community. The experts arrive, he says, with readymade answers, carrying out projects which may be well-intended but which basically disturb people's lives, after which they leave complaining about the lack of gratitude on the part of African people. As he put it in the metaphorical language typical of his style: "If you are told to cover a dead body with a cloth, you may take any colour. But if the dead person were alive, you should first have asked him whether or not he accepts this or that colour."[23] Development projects, he has always believed, should begin with the people concerned. But it is not only Westerners who should be blamed, in his view. The African political elite, who have made it their business to exploit their own people and keep them poor, are equally guilty. Hence things have not much improved since independence, and this has contributed to the current deplorable state of affairs on the continent. Milingo has described the transition from colonial rule to independent government as one of coming out of the mouth of the lion and going into the leopard's mouth. "The poor man is not safe, he dies all the same, because both these animals are carnivorous."[24]

Milingo's views of development have changed little since he started to reflect systematically on the matter in the 1970s. His starting point, the dignity of man, has remained unaltered. As early as 1976, he described what nowadays all and sundry seem to agree on: how Africa has been turned into a continent of beggars and made dependent to an alarming degree on Western development aid. To his mind, this is largely due to the predominant Western attitude, which defines development purely in terms of material progress and has turned Africans into consumers. Human development, he insists, cannot simply be equated with the material progress of a nation, and the latter should not be seen as a criterion of civilization: "Wearing a suit does not necessarily exclude one from the membership of bandits."[25]

More recently, after the turbulent events of 2001 when he publicly aligned himself with the church of Reverend Moon, and following his subsequent (but not lasting) reconciliation with the Church, the archbishop has once again devoted his attention to the issue of development in Africa. This time he has combined his theories with actual practice in his home country, Zambia. This provides an interesting example of the way development theory can depart from the daily experiences of the people concerned, in this case ordinary Zambians. Milingo has dubbed his theory the Mbuliuli Economic Principle, the details of which he has elaborated in three booklets that have been organized almost in the form of short instruction books for users.[26] Mbuliuli is the name of the maize that is the staple diet for most Zambians, "the maize which bursts and takes a new form (pop corn)."[27] In the creative mind of Milingo it is turned into a leading principle of a homemade economic theory based on the wisdom of the ancestors, which, he realizes, is not going to make "a soft landing" in professional economic circles. Although it is a very practical theory, in its core it is based on the fundamental belief (referred to above) that economic prosperity is linked to inner growth, or, that economic expansion goes hand in hand with "expansion from within."

Self-reliance and sufficiency are the core elements in Milingo's approach, with the money earned being plowed back into the country to be invested there. To that end, he fills conventional economic terms with new meanings that are connected with the cultural knowledge of ordinary Zambians (ancestral wisdom) and do justice to their religious worldview (traditional and Christian in this case), as well as being presented in their local language. Thus, he introduces new terms, in the local language and explained in English, such as fluid money and capital donation, and referring to the local community that owns the means of production as a Moral Entity. The head of a Mbuliuli Enterprise (of which there exist several now) is the "caretaker" of the business, which is characterized by joint ownership. Apart from being innovative, the mbuliuli approach is another typical expression of the belief that for lasting effect one must start at the individual level. The underlying idea is to create a new business spirit and help Zambia arrive at self-reliance rather than being dependent on the exploitative business of foreign investors that leaves the country poor.[28] Most of all, the approach recognizes that development is intrinsically connected to human dignity, of a country and of its citizens.

Human Development

Development is today widely understood as *human* development, which broadens the concept to include aspects beyond the economic meaning that often used to be exclusively ascribed to it.[29] This broader understanding allows for a different approach by foreign development workers and donors, so that it empowers people to develop the full range of resources at their disposal. These include religious or spiritual resources.[30] This begs the question whether there is an insurmountable divide between a spiritually driven approach and the more material approach Western organizations are familiar with. The latter often doubt that models based on religion will be able to respond to the material needs of people in developing countries. It is widely agreed, however, that human development must build on people's own resources. Thus we must ask ourselves what can be done to mobilize people's religious or spiritual resources to realize human development in the broadest sense.

There is neither a good reason nor a rational argument to justify the neglect of an important human resource if and when it appears to be available. This includes not only material and intellectual but also religious and spiritual resources. The latter, too, produce knowledge, perhaps less tangible but in many cases of a sort that is, or can be made, beneficial to the community. Religious resources, I have argued elsewhere, can analytically be distinguished into four vital categories: religious ideas, religious practices, religious organization, and religious experiences.[31] Each of these can be explored for its development potential. So far, it is mostly the organizational structures religion produces that have received attention. While these are of obvious importance, given the basis of trust that usually binds people belonging to the same community in economic and social activities, it is not enough. It is notably the inspiration people derive from their religious ideology that needs to be exploited. The active communication with a spirit world from which believers derive their power, and the evident collaboration between the human and spirit worlds to which they aspire, can actually become an important resource for development.[32]

For religious believers in Africa, spiritual power is real and "enabling power." By interacting with a spirit world they get access to, and may share in, a form of power that can transform their lives. Spiritual empowerment, as we may call this process, also has certain consequences for the way in which people consider development projects. Their religious understanding of development connects success and progress in the material world with spiritual growth and inner progress. This is a message that today is also spread by African Christians living and working in Europe, as part of their evangelistic mission in the West. This will be the subject of the final chapter.

Chapter Seven
A Valley of Dry Bones:
African Christians Going Global

It has become common among Western observers to refer to the present religious dynamism in Africa as a form of "re-enchantment," suggesting that Africa has reversed a trend of secularization that originated during the colonial period and was perpetuated in postcolonial times. The disenchantment of the world is seen as a natural process and an inevitable outcome of historical evolution. In the case of Africa (and other parts of the non-Western world) this appears to be a wrong assumption, entirely based on an analysis of processes in European history.

The idea of re-enchantment is taken from the work of Max Weber, one of the founding fathers of sociology. Writing around a century ago, Weber introduced the idea of disenchantment (*Entzäuberung*) as one of the key characteristics of the European societies of his time. European scholars have often applied Eurocentric analyses to Africa, in the belief, implicit or explicit, that the history of their own continent offers a guide for progress and development elsewhere. In Africa, this approach obscures the vitality of religion as a constitutive element of the continent's societies, past and present. We should be aware of the fallacy of taking concepts derived from an often idealized reading of European history, and of assuming they can be applied to societies in all parts of the world without further consideration of historical context and specificities. The notion of "re-enchantment," therefore, is an unhelpful application of Weber's original idea about the course of European history. Since Africa has never been disenchanted in a Weberian sense, it stands to reason that it cannot be re-enchanted either. A re-enchantment of Africa appears to be taking place only in the perception of observers who themselves have become disenchanted over the years as a result of the secularization of their own societies, notably in western Europe.

Moreover, religious developments in Africa must be seen in a global context. To some extent, the perceived revival of religion in many parts of the former colonial world can be said to reflect reaction to modernization and development as these have been historically experienced. We may see that, after years of colonial rule, during which the secular option was presented as viable for the governance of communities, society is reconnecting with its precolonial past.[1] A similar observation can be made regarding Muslim societies in the Middle East. What often appears to external observers as a religious revival is better analyzed as a form of historical continuity of contemporary societies with their own past. The "re-enchantment" of Africa in the form of a perceived revival of religion can be seen as part of this process. It testifies to the continuing vitality of Africa's indigenous religious traditions, which have been able to renew and reform themselves throughout history, and are now doing so once more.[2]

Africa's spirit-oriented religious traditions can today be found everywhere, in proselytization by African Christians and Muslims, but also in the transformation of African "traditional" religions into aspiring world religions. Rosalind Hackett has identified the following five tendencies in the twentieth-century process of revitalization of African traditional religions: universalization, modernization, commercialization, politicization, and individualization.[3] These can all be seen as resulting from a process of migration that has long taken Africans overseas. Originally, this was to a large extent a consequence of the trans-Atlantic slave trade, which gave rise, for example, to the emergence of new religions such as Umbanda and Candomblé. Yoruba religion, originally from Nigeria, is now a well-known phenomenon on both sides of the Atlantic. But in modern times, too, we can observe how African religions—whether they originated in Africa itself, like African traditional religions, or were originally imports to Africa, such as Christianity and Islam—have traveled overseas. As a result of new migration patterns African religious traditions have now reached many parts of the Western world, including Europe, where many vibrant African Christian and Muslim communities exist. What appears to some as a form of re-enchantment is in fact a recent expression of the dynamics of change that have always characterized Africa's various religious traditions.

African Christians in Europe

African-initiated churches now exist in every part of the world where Africans have settled. As far back as the early 1990s, the General Post Office in Accra had introduced a special postal service to a number of European countries where a significant number of Ghanaians lived. These included not only such an obvious destination as the United Kingdom, but also the Netherlands, Germany, France, Belgium, and Switzerland. Outside Europe the most popular destinations appeared to be the United States, Canada, and, surprisingly, Japan. However, the present chapter focuses on Europe.[4]

The emergence and spread of African-initiated churches outside the African continent may be seen as a sign of the tendency to universalization mentioned in the previous section with regard to Africa's indigenous religions. This time it is related to one of the most remarkable trends of our time, the scope and size of international migration, including migration from sub-Saharan Africa. In the last two to three decades, African immigrants have spread over virtually all industrialized countries of western and northern Europe. One unexpected result has been the foundation of new Christian congregations in all the places where the immigrants have settled. African Christians have truly gone global in recent years, with Europe a significant outpost.

African Christians in Europe are a relative novelty, certainly in comparison to the United States, where, due to the slave trade, African Christians have long existed and have made a considerable contribution to religious history. Black Christianity, as this trend is generally known, has been part and parcel of religious life in America for centuries. This is different in Europe, even though an exception has to be made for Africa's former colonizing powers—notably Britain and France—which have had a significant presence of Africans since the 1960s, when most African countries became independent. Britain particularly has been home to African Christian communities since that time. Other European countries, which had fewer prior links with sub-Saharan Africa, such as the Netherlands, Germany, and Italy, have now become popular destinations for Africans trying to escape political or economic conditions in their home countries. The economic and political crises in Africa in the 1980s drastically altered existing patterns of migration, turning Africans increasingly away from the continent. Poverty, human rights violations, and the absence of peace and security have caused African people to move away from their continent of birth and settle elsewhere.

Among the recent immigrants to Europe are many people from Ghana, the majority of whom are Christian adherents and largely responsible for the foundation of numerous new Christian congregations in Europe. Others have been founded by people from Nigeria, the Democratic Republic of Congo (DRC), and Angola, to mention some of the most prominent. They are notably present in prosperous countries such as Germany, the Netherlands, Italy, Belgium, and France, where Sunday services are held in a great variety of African languages, including Twi (Ghana), Lingala (DRC), Yoruba (Nigeria), and Tigrinya (Ethiopia), increasingly combined with the national language of the relevant country of immigration.

Thus churches founded by Africans (African-initiated churches) exist now all over Europe. Many, if not most, of these have been founded as congregations independent of the mainline churches in the host country. Outsiders commonly refer to these new churches as "African churches," a label often rejected by the churches themselves on the grounds that it marks a restriction of their task and mission in Europe; as far as they are concerned, they aim to minister to Africans and non-Africans, black and white people. Most label themselves "international churches," expressing their aspiration to be part of the international world in which they believe they have a universal task. Europeans often tend to overlook the international aspirations of African congregations, on the grounds that their membership is largely black, but Africans view this matter differently. One unexpected and, to many Europeans, surprising aspect of African Christian congregations is their view of Western society, which is almost a mirror image of conventional Western views of Africa. Many of the tens of thousands of African Christians who live in Europe regard Western society as a place where people have abandoned God. In their view, Europe is a spiritual wasteland that can be made fertile again with help from Africa. Just as European missionaries once believed in their divine task of bringing the gospel to Africa, African church leaders in Europe are convinced of their mission to bring the gospel back to those who originally provided them with it.

For many African Christians, therefore, migration to Europe is seen not just as an economic necessity, but as a God-given opportunity to evangelize among those whom they believe to have gone astray. Europe is like the "valley of dry bones" described in the vision of the prophet Ezekiel (Ezek. 37: 1–14), who laments the decay of Israel and foresees its revival. Ezekiel, the prophet of the exile period, is depicted in the Old Testament as a seer of doom. But he is also the prophet of good news who foresees the rebirth of the people of God in a vision of salvation. In his vision, the spirit of God leads Ezekiel around a valley where the ground is covered with bones, and he sees that there are very many and also very dry. God speaks to Ezekiel and asks him: "Mortal man, can these bones come back to life?" Ezekiel has no answer, stating that only God will know. Ezekiel is subsequently told to prophesy to the dry bones and tell them to listen to the word of God. Only then will they be able to regain life.

The message contained in the metaphor as used by African Christians in Europe is clear: Europe will be dependent on Africa for renewed spiritual vitality. Many Africans in Europe see in the vision of the prophet Ezekiel a compelling resemblance to Christianity in the Western world. Due to secularization, western Europe has become a spiritual desert, a valley of dry bones stripped of flesh and spirit. Europe is spiritually dead. It can come back to life only if somebody will prophesy and, following Ezekiel's example, tell these dry bones to listen to the word of God: a task African Christians have taken upon themselves. Hence, a reverse mission has been set in motion.

The need for a reverse mission in Europe is often implied in the vision or mission statement of these new churches. In the Netherlands in the 1990s, for example, the congregation of the United Assemblies of God International developed a mission program titled "The Valley Vision," in reference to Ezekiel's valley of dry bones. The vision of these congregations is usually also expressed in the church name, as the example shows. Hence, we find African congregations with names such as Lighthouse Chapel International, Word Miracle Church International, Church of Rock International, Compassion Ministries International, or New Anointing Ministries Worldwide. The same is true of some of the umbrella organizations, such as GATE, one of the first organized African missions in the Netherlands, which originally stood for Gospel from Africa to Europe, but was later changed to Gift from Africa to Europe.

Missionaries are often sent by a mother church in the country of origin, such as the Nigerian Redeemed Christian Church of God (RCCG), one of the largest independent churches in Nigeria, which has branches in almost forty European countries. It has stated its aim to build a Christian congregation within five minutes travel from anywhere in the world.[4] The Church of Pentecost in Ghana has many branches in Europe, led from its mission department at church headquarters in Accra. One of its mission reports refers to the "deadening traditionalism, formalism and theological disputes" in the Netherlands, which are considered to hamper the missionary task of the church.[5] Eastern Europe, too, has become a fertile area for African missionaries. A highly successful example is Nigerian pastor Sunday Adelaja, a former student in Moscow, who has founded a thriving church in Ukraine known as the Embassy of God Church. Unlike most similar churches in western Europe, it is attended by thousands of mostly white members.[6] A comparable trend in missionary activity from Africa may be seen in the increasing number of African Catholic priests who minister in Europe, which is suffering from a lack of priestly vocations.

The founding of this new wave of African-initiated churches on the

European continent has happened within a relative short period. In Britain such churches have been in existence since the 1960s because of its former colonial ties, but elsewhere in Europe the rise of African congregations marks the opening of a rather newer chapter in the religious history of the European continent. Although the continuing lack of systematic research into the spread of these new churches prevents us from stating with certainty how many there are and precisely where, we know from the little research that has been done that African-initiated churches exist in most of the countries in the European Union. We are speaking in this case of Christian groups that demonstrate some organized structure, and which may vary significantly in size, from some dozen to hundreds of worshippers, or, as in the Ukrainian example, several thousands. They do not include the many prayer groups and similar structures that tend to congregate in private homes or otherwise operate outside the public view. Due to the secularized nature of the host societies, most of these new churches have great difficulty to find a physical place for worship. Depending on their size, they often congregate in places not originally intended for that purpose, such as community buildings, derelict shops, or premises tucked away under the car parks of the large apartment blocks that have become a common feature of modern life in Europe's suburban quarters.

The emergence of African congregations in Europe also marks a new phase in the history of African independent churches. In the course of time, scholars and others have applied a wide range of different labels to these churches. They have become known as "spiritual churches," "healing churches," or simply "independent churches" or "African churches." A difficulty is that these labels often reflect more than anything else the subjective view of outside observers, who are struck by a particular feature that is not common in their own tradition, whether this is a spirit orientation, an emphasis on healing, or indeed a supposed exclusive "African-ness." Thus the name "African Independent Churches" is not self-chosen but a label originally imposed by outsiders, representatives of the historical mainline churches or former mission churches that until a century or so ago held a monopoly in church development in Africa. The "I" for "independent" originally reflected the mainline church viewpoint that these churches had broken away from the missionary-led mother churches. In the twentieth century, a shift in influence from mainline to so-called independent churches expressed itself in the AICs' self-chosen name, African Indigenous Churches. The change of name is not just a play with words but reflects a change of emphasis from outsider to insider. In the insider's view, the aspect of separation from a mother church is not relevant; the crucial point is the establishment of a self-image by creating one's own identity.

In the course of time new appellations emerging from within the AICs themselves have further altered the meaning of the letter "I." Thus AICs have also become known as African Instituted Churches and African Initiated Churches, representing different historical angles from which the phenomenon can be viewed, while retaining the acronym. This shows the outside world that most, if not all, churches in Africa are today under the leadership of Africans, including the former mission churches in Africa.

Using the same acronym but interpreting the "I" with different words shows how the status of these churches changed over the twentieth century. The name changes are an eloquent statement of the dynamics of this history. The new African-initiated churches in Europe, I have suggested in my book *Halfway to Paradise*, represent a new type of AICs. To do justice to the historical change implied in the worldwide spread of African-initiated churches, I have proposed to invest the initials "AIC" with a new meaning, African International Churches. To refer to them this way takes account of their African origin, while recognizing their continuity with the universal Christian tradition. In any event, and most important, this outlook accords with that of members of the churches themselves, who are conscious of having entered the international field.

This point takes us back to the importance of identity and self-identity notably discussed in Chapter 2, and to the question who has the power to define identity. I have argued elsewhere that the definition of identity should result from a process of negotiation in which the people concerned participate. Obviously, the mechanisms for this are influenced by the size of a particular minority group vis-à-vis the majority population. Africans in Europe are a relatively small minority and have little or no power as a group. This can also be said of African Christians in Europe, whose churches are normally not included in the established church structures in their country of residence. Hence, they are often seen in exclusive terms as "African" Christians, rather than as Christians who happen to have their roots in Africa. Their churches are seen as ethnic churches, rather than as Christian churches like others in the host countries. For Christian migrants from Africa, religious identity is more significant than ethnic identity, according to research conducted in the Netherlands. The experience of exclusion from the religious mainstream, however, may well encourage them in the future to reconsider their self-identity specifically as "African" Christians. This has been the case, for example, in the United Kingdom, where, in a very different context, African and

Afro-Caribbean church leaders tend to insist on their African identity in the experience of their faith.[7]

International Migration

The background against which the changing relations between churches in Europe and Africa should be considered, we have noted, is that of international migration. Although this is not a new phenomenon in itself, its present scope and scale are unprecedented, a largely unforeseen byproduct of globalization. In the mid-1990s, when European migration policies began to change significantly, the total migrant population in the world was estimated at 130 million, including refugees.[8] This implies that large numbers of people in the world are living in a country other than that of their birth. In the late 1980s it was estimated that more than 20 million people in western Europe had been born in a country other than the one in which they then lived.[9] Immigration, thus, has become a permanent feature of society.

Migration patterns have changed enormously in Europe since World War II, when western Europe changed from a net zone of emigration to one of immigration. Whereas before 1940 Europeans were frequently emigrants themselves, after the war northern European governments began to recruit labor migrants from the Mediterranean basin in particular to help in the economic reconstruction of their devastated countries. These migrants, often from predominantly Muslim countries, introduced Islam into western Europe. Because the economic reconstruction of Europe in the postwar era almost coincided with the independence of former colonies in the 1950s and 1960s, migration from what was then called the Third World also became much more frequent. South-north migration increased significantly during the 1970s when important economic changes were taking place worldwide. After the fall of the Berlin Wall in 1989, which marked the end of the Cold War, international migration was further stimulated. Since that time, European countries assembled in the European Union have enacted new laws to control international migration in an attempt to counter and reshape this trend.

One remarkable feature in recent immigration patterns is the numbers of people coming to Europe from increasingly farther south. Available statistics suggest that, in the mid-1990s in the then fifteen EU member states, the total number of immigrants registered from countries in Africa, Asia, and South and Central America amounted to 5.6 million, including asylum-seekers, but not including the large numbers of undocumented migrants, among whom were substantial numbers of Africans. Africa continues to rank high among the continents of origin of non-European immigrants, to such a degree that European governments have taken draconian measures to try and halt their numbers. One of the most striking features of European politics today is the attempt to erect barriers—even literally[10]—between Europe and Africa, with the aim of preventing Africans from even trying to settle in the West. Even more striking is the emergence of a Europe-wide official policy based on a consensus that the proper place for Africans is in Africa, not Europe, with exceptions for highly skilled personnel such as doctors, nurses, and footballers. But the reports of young African men and women trying to reach Europe at the risk of losing their lives on the way are numerous and their images well known. Human trade and trafficking, as is widely known among politicians and other policy makers, has become one of the most lucrative businesses of our time.

Poverty is widely considered one of the root causes of migration. It appears to be the main reason many young Africans have left for Europe, and continue to do so in spite of the difficulties they encounter on the way. Particularly among these immigrants who come to Europe to seek work, there are many undocumented migrants, people who lack the legal papers that permit them to stay in the country of their choice and who are popularly known as "illegals." It is impossible, for obvious reasons, to establish exactly how many undocumented migrants are living in the various countries of western Europe. Recent estimates suggest that there are several million, in addition to the estimated 18 million legal migrants working and living in the continent. The International Labour Organization proposes a figure of 2.6 million undocumented migrants, but other estimates are much higher. The stringent measures by European governments to reduce the number of immigrants make it increasingly difficult for them to legalize their presence. Many live clandestinely, without any official registration, in the hope of better times to come. They may join one of the African-initiated churches, becoming part of a community network that will help them in their struggle for survival, both spiritually and materially.

The foundation of new Christian congregations in all the places where Africans have settled is an unintended and unexpected result of African migration to Europe in the last two decades. They vary from simple house congregations to churches with large memberships. These churches are adding a new and significant element to the religious landscape of European countries.

African International Churches

The increasing presence of African-initiated churches in Europe poses a number of challenges to existing churches there, notably at the levels of theology (usually spirit-oriented) and church organization (often charisma-based). In many of these newly founded churches, charismatic leadership provides the basis of organization because of the importance attached to personal vocation. This element is even more prominent in cases where the church leader is regarded as a prophet. In the Netherlands, with its strong emphasis on egalitarianism, charismatic leadership not only differs fundamentally from the conventional Dutch church pattern but is often frowned upon as a symptom of undemocratic leadership and therefore not readily accepted. When during a church exchange visit elections of new officers took place in the Dutch congregation, the visiting African Christians were shocked at first, as this did not comply with their view of charisma-based election. The phrase "God is not a democrat"[11] is an apt representation of such a view. Another striking difference from traditional churches in Europe is the large variety of offices for which African-led churches draw their inspiration directly from the Bible. Most churches, especially those of the pentecostal type, recognize the ministries mentioned in the New Testament that played an important role at the time of the formation of the early church, namely, apostle, prophet, evangelist, pastor, and teacher. The leadership of an AIC in Europe often consists of a board with a varying number of functionaries, in which the head pastor is usually the most influential person in policy- and decision-making. Spiritual training is an important characteristic. Officials charged with carrying out specific tasks prepare themselves by Bible study, prayer, and fasting. Every task performed on behalf of the church is believed to contribute to the coming of the kingdom of God on earth and therefore considered a serious duty.

At the level of theology there are a number of differences between the new African international churches and the European mainstream ones. These differences are characteristic of the Black Church tradition. In Chapter 2 I referred to Walter Hollenweger to point out some significant features, including the orality of liturgy and the narrativity of theology; the participatory character of the services and of church life more generally; the importance of dreams and visions; and the specific understanding of the body-mind relationship, which becomes particularly clear in the importance attached to healing through prayer.[12] In addition there is a widespread belief in the actual presence and instrumentality of spiritual forces, which may be considered either good or evil. Evil, as we saw in Chapter 3, is believed to manifest itself through spiritual agencies, in the form of evil spirits, or through human be-ings, in the case of "witches" (see Chapter 5). To counter evil forces, African Christians call on the power of the Holy Spirit. Spiritual empowerment pre-supposes belief in a spiritual world or a world of spirits, which African Chris-tians believe to be also the Holy Spirit's abode. African Christians in Europe, too, have a strong belief in the power of the Spirit as a force in their lives that may be evoked immediately. For them, the Holy Spirit is a real, personal, and tangible force, a view that differs from that most common in Western philo-sophical and theological traditions. The difference, I have consistently argued in this book, stems from the type of cosmology underlying the intellectual construction of reality in Africa and Europe respectively.

Typical problems for which African Christians in Europe seek a solu-tion with the help of the Holy Spirit are those related to the need for legal documents such as a residence or work permit, marriage difficulties, or prob-lems with the education of children. These obviously arise from the difficult circumstances created by migration. Their European counterparts not only stand in a different tradition, but also are generally free from social pres-sures of this sort. Witchcraft belief is another area where African Christians in Europe often are in need of spiritual guidance and action.[13] One need only refer to reports in the British press, as mentioned in Chapter 5, to realize the seriousness of this matter. African Christians in Europe also do other types of work in their communities, which is sometimes of great social importance. For example, Tom Marfo, the Ghanaian pastor of one of the new churches in the large migrant district of Amsterdam, is also the founder of CARF, the Christian Aid and Resources Foundation, devoted to the fight against human trafficking in the Netherlands. It supports women who have fallen victim to such practices, including many African women who have ended up in pros-titution.[14] In 2002, Marfo was awarded a prestigious prize for his important humanitarian work in the Netherlands, which is entirely based on his reli-gious inspiration.

The Bible remains the most important spiritual *and* intellectual re-source for African Christians. The inclusive model of human society which African international churches derive from their understanding of the Bible stands in stark contrast to their actual experience of European society, which tends to exclude perceived outsiders. The place accorded to Bible reading is a significant point of distinction between African and Western Christians in general. African Christians carry their Bible with them; they make notes in the margins, underline important passages to re-read and study at home, or take notes in separate notebooks. The close attention to biblical texts may be seen as the reappropriation of what they consider the true word of God. Such reading of the Bible leads them also to develop an analysis of what, in their view, are the faults of European society and what should be done to redress them. Their political critique is couched in a spirit idiom. It is therefore implicit and not easily recognized as such by the host society. When African Christians state that the Bible shows that God does not recognize any borders, or that God is able to move mountains, they mean what they say, calling on the power of the Holy Spirit to make the impossible happen. They apply ideas and theories drawn from the Bible to build themselves spiritually and intellectually, as knowledge of the Bible is believed to open the way to self-knowledge and for people to discover who they really are, namely (in their own words) "children of God." Here, too, we see how the spiritual dimension of humankind is considered crucial to its existence (as suggested in a different way in the chapter on human rights), underlining the perceived indivisibility of life characteristic of African religiosity generally.

African Christians in Europe may be socially and politically marginalized and lacking influence, but spiritually they are self-confident and aspiring. They do not hesitate to witness to their faith in public, emphasizing the value of personal evangelization. Today it has become common to see African missionaries preaching in public places in the big cities of Europe, Bible in hand. African Christians seem to have little doubt about the eventual success of their undertaking: the reconversion of Europe. Their ideas on this matter have probably been shaped also by stories or memories of the original success of European missionaries in Africa.

This reversal of roles, implied in the notion of a reverse mission—from Africa to Europe this time—is not accepted easily by Europeans, however, as it stands many conventional ideas on their head. Europeans generally see Africans as on the receiving end, and themselves on the giving end, of a well-defined relationship, as we saw in the discussion on development. Africans are not people from whom Europeans expect something in return. This position is also reflected in the attitude of many Western churches, which find it difficult to accept that African Christians might have something to teach *them*. There is often little awareness in Europe of the contribution African Christians could make to church life in general. This attitude presumably stems from early missionary prejudice as well as from the general idea that still holds: Africans are essentially people to be helped.

The many African Christians who think that Europe has become a spiritual desert conceive of themselves as bringing the solution. It is interesting to note that they have reversed the Western missionary tradition not only in purely religious terms, but also in a broader sense of bringing relief to people perceived as being in need. In this particular case, Africans, rightly or wrongly, consider the poverty they find in Europe to be spiritual in nature, rather than a material deprivation. From the perspective of African Christians, by their evangelical work, they might actually be contributing to what they hope will become the "re-enchantment" of Europe. At present, it is far from clear what lasting influence African Christians in Europe may have, and what will be the future effects not only of their missionary efforts, but also of their very presence. If some form of re-conversion were to come about, Christians in Europe might recall the vision of the prophet Ezekiel, as they need not say, like the mortal man quoted there, that "they are dried up, without any hope and with no future" (Ezek. 37: 11).

*   *   *

Rather than becoming weaker or otherwise declining in importance, the religious traditions of Africa have emerged strong and vital from their encounter with the outside world. As this book has shown, African Christianity reflects a strong element of continuity with the continent's original religious traditions. In particular, African understandings of Christianity are marked by the belief in a dynamic spiritual universe. This pattern of understanding is a social fact that should impose itself on any coherent analysis. Hence, for a Western analyst such as myself, it becomes important to render conventional Western ideas concerning religion in Africa in a symbolic language that takes African realities into account, rather than simply applying the vocabulary and concepts that conventionally underlie Western secular thought. As I have argued in this book, this observation also applies to matters of great contemporary importance that Western observers often do not associate with religion, including human rights and development.

Since the middle of the twentieth century, the decline of Christianity in Europe and its simultaneous expansion in Africa have brought about a reversal of the religious roles of the two continents. In recent decades, this process has been strengthened by the rise of African migration worldwide. Africa is now a major player in world Christianity, and has become conscious of a reversal of roles regarding the West. If it is difficult to predict what effect this will have on Africa, it is even more difficult to predict the long-term impact on Western societies, particularly in Europe. What is clear in any event is that the Christian God has already become African.

Notes

Chapter 1. God in Africa: Some Key Issues

1. A definition particularly associated with German-American theologian Paul Tillich. See Tillich, *Theology of Culture* (New York: Oxford University Press, 1959).

2. Italo Ronca, "What's in Two Names: Old and New Thoughts on the History and Etymology of *Religio* and *Superstitio*," in Serafino Prete, ed., *Respublica Literarum: Studies in the Classical Tradition* 15, 1 (1992): 43–60.

3. Cf. Tomoko Masuzawa, "Theory Without Method: Situating a Discourse Analysis on Religion," in Gerrie ter Haar and Yoshio Tsuruoka, eds., *Religion and Society: An Agenda for the 21st Century* (Leiden: Brill, 2007), 173–204.

4. Edward Burnett Tylor, *Primitive Culture*, 1871; reprinted in two volumes: *The Origins of Culture* and *Religion in Primitive Culture* (New York: Harper, 1958). Note that the concept of culture has been defined and employed in a great variety of ways and that there is no overall consensus as to its precise meaning.

5. Gerrie ter Haar, *Spirit of Africa: The Healing Ministry of Archbishop Milingo of Zambia* (London: Hurst; Trenton: Africa World Press, 1992), which analyzes the conflict in detail.

6. Erika Bourguignon, "Introduction: A Framework for the Comparative Study of Altered States of Consciousness," in Erika Bourguignon, ed., *Religion, Altered States of Consciousness, and Social Change* (Columbus: Ohio State University Press, 1973), 3–35.

7. Cf. Felicitas D. Goodman, *How About Demons? Possession and Exorcism in the Modern World* (Bloomington: Indiana University Press, 1988).

8. See Rupert Sheldrake's homepage at http://www.sheldrake.org/homepage.html.

9. Rupert Sheldrake, *A New Science of Life: The Hypothesis of Formative Causation* (Los Angeles: Tarcher, 1981), and *The Presence of the Past: Morphic Resonance and the Habits of Nature* (New York: Times Books, 1988).

10. Roger Penrose, *The Emperor's New Mind: Concerning Computers, Minds and the Laws of Physics* (Oxford: Oxford University Press, 1989). This was followed in 1994 by *Shadows of the Mind: A Search for the Missing Science of Consciousness* (Oxford: Oxford University Press, 1994).

11. David J. Chalmers, *The Conscious Mind: In Search of a Fundamental Theory* (New York: Oxford University Press, 1996).

12. Pim van Lommel, *Eindeloos Bewustzijn: Een Wetenschappelijke Visie op de Bijna-Dood Ervaring* (Endless Consciousness: A Scientific View of the Near-Death Experience) (Kampen: Ten Have, 2007).

13. Pim van Lommel, Ruud van Wees, Vincent Meyers, and Ingrid Elfferich, "Near-Death Experience in Survivors of Cardiac Arrest: A Prospective Study in the Netherlands," *The Lancet* 358 (2001): 2039–45.

14. Danah Zohar and Ian Marshall, *Spiritual Capital: Wealth We Can Live By* (London: Bloomsbury, 2004), 95.

15. Similar developments have occurred at earlier periods. For example, in colonial Mexico the Black Virgin of Guadelupe had an indigenous physiognomy, wore indigenous ornaments, and spoke a local language. She became known as "the Evangelizer of the Americas." See Virgilio P. Elizondo, *La Morenita: Evangelizer of the Americas* (San Antonio: Mexican American Cultural Center, 1980).

16. See the critical discussion in Celestine Nyamu-Musembi and Andrea Cornwall, "What Is the 'Rights-Based Approach' All About? Perspectives from International Development Agencies," IDS Working Paper 234, Institute of Development Studies, Brighton, Sussex, November 2004, notably 1, 14.

17. Ibid., 1.

18. See the United Nations Development Programme (UNDP) website, http://hdr.undp.org/.

19. Zbigniew Brzezinski, *Out of Control: Global Turmoil on the Eve of the Twenty-First Century* (New York: Scribner, 1993), 17.

20. Emmanuel Milingo, *Development: An African View* (Box Hill, Victoria: Scripture Keys Ministries, 1994). This was first produced in mimeograph in 1976.

21. Ibid., 3.

22. Ibid., 4.

23. Gerrie ter Haar, *Halfway to Paradise: African Christians in Europe* (Cardiff: Cardiff Academic Press, 1998).

Chapter 2. How God Became African: A Continuing Story

1. Elizabeth Isichei, *A History of Christianity in Africa: From Antiquity to the Present* (Grand Rapids, Mich.: Eerdmans; Lawrenceville, N.J.: Africa World Press, 1995), 1.

2. Isichei (1) gives an estimate number of 400 million. In their "Annual Statistical Table on Global Mission: 2004," *International Bulletin of Missionary Research* 28, 1 (2004): 25, David B. Barrett and Todd M. Johnson provide a lower number of around 350 million, but they estimate an increase to 640 million in 2025.

3. David B. Barrett and Todd M. Johnson, "Annual Statistical Table on Global Mission: 2008," *International Bulletin of Missionary Research* 32, 1 (2008): 30.

4. Ibid. According to these prognoses only Latin America would have slightly more Christian adherents: 634,345,000, versus 627,557,000 for Africa and 474,745,000 for Asia.

5. The latter includes Russia, where the growth of Christian churches since the end of the Cold War has been spectacular.

6. Kwame Bediako, *Christianity in Africa: The Renewal of a Non-Western Religion* (Edinburgh: Edinburgh University Press, 1995).

7. As commonly suggested in Western media.

8. The initials AIC have been given different meanings in the course of history. See Chapter 7 for further discussion.

9. Bennetta W. Jules-Rosette, "Tradition and Continuity in African Religions: The Case of New Religious Movements," in Jacob K. Olupona, ed., *African Traditional Religions in Contemporary Soc*iety (New York: Paragon House, 1991), 149–65.

10. E.g., Allan H. Anderson, "Types and Butterflies: African Initiated Churches and European Typologies," *International Bulletin of Missionary Research* 25, 3 (2001): 107–13.

11. See ibid., 150–51.

12. Gerhardus C. Oosthuizen, "The African Independent Churches' Centenary," *Africa Insight* 15, 2 (1985): 70. The Thembu Church, established in 1884 in South Africa, is usually considered the first independent church in sub-Saharan Africa (71).

13. Gerrie ter Haar, *World Religions and Community Religions: Where Does Africa Fit In?* Occasional Paper, Centre of African Studies (Copenhagen: University of Copenhagen, 2000).

14. See Gerrie ter Haar, *Halfway to Paradise: African Christians in Europe* (Cardiff: Cardiff Academic Press, 1998).

15. Gerrie ter Haar, *Spirit of Africa: The Healing Ministry of Archbishop Milingo of Zambia* (London: Hurst; Trenton, N.J.: Africa World Press, 1992) provides an examination of his conflict with the Church of Rome.

16. Emmanuel Milingo, *Liberation Through Christ: African Point of View*, lectures given at Divine Word Centre, London, Ontario (Canada), 12–16 April 1977 (mimeographed), 8.

17. For an analysis, see Ter Haar, *Spirit of Africa*, chap. 2.

18. Emmanuel Milingo, *The Demarcations* (Lusaka: Teresianum Press, 1982), 116.

19. In a Tillich-like manner; see Chapter 1.

20. Terence O. Ranger, "African Traditional Religion," in Stewart Sutherland and Peter Clarke, eds., *The Study of Religion, Traditional and New Religions* (London: Routledge, 1991), 106–14.

21. Stephen Ellis and Gerrie ter Haar, *Worlds of Power: Religious Thought and Political Practice in Africa* (London: Hurst; New York: Oxford University Press, 2004).

22. Ranger, "African Traditional Religion."

23. Cephas N. Omenyo, *Pentecost Outside Pentecostalism: A Study of the Development of Charismatic Renewal in the Mainline Churches in Ghana* (Zoetermeer: Boekencentrum, 2002).

24. Walter J. Hollenweger, "Priorities in Pentecostal Research: Historiography, Missiology, Hermeneutics and Pneumatology," in Jan A. B. Jongeneel, ed., *Experiences of the Spirit: Conference on Pentecostal and Charismatic Research in Europe at Utrecht University 1989* (Frankfurt/M.: Peter Lang, 1991), 7–22.

25. See Ter Haar, *Spirit of Africa*, 177–82.

26. Birgit Meyer, "Christianity in Africa: From African Independent to Pentecostal-Charismatic Churches," *Annual Review of Anthropology* 33 (2004): 447–74.

27. Sally Falk Moore, *Anthropology and Africa: Changing Perspectives on a Changing Scene*, (Charlottesville: University Press of Virginia, 1994), 129.

19. Rian Malan, *My Traitor's Heart: A South African Exile Returns to Face His Country, His Tribe, and His Conscience* (London: Bodley Head, 1990), 159–83.

20. Jack Nandi, "The Jerusalem Church of Christ: A Historical and Theological Analysis," MA thesis, Department of Religion, University of Nairobi, 1993.

21. J. M. Schoffeleers, "Christ as the Medicine-Man and the Medicine-Man as Christ: A Tentative History of African Christological Thought," *Man and Life* 8, 1, 2 (1982): 11–28.

22. For a scholarly discussion of these examples, see Heike Behrend, *Alice Lakwena and the Holy Spirits: War in Northern Uganda, 1986–97* (Oxford: James Currey, 1999); Stephen Ellis, *The Mask of Anarchy: The Destruction of Liberia and the Religious Dimension of an African Civil War* (London: Hurst; New York: New York University Press, 1999).

Chapter 4. African Religious Experiences: From Suffering to Salvation

1. Cf. Thomas W. Overholt, *Channels of Prophecy: The Social Dynamics of Prophetic Activity* (Minneapolis: Fortress Press, 1989).

2 An expression taken from Tshenuwani Simon Farisani, *Dagboek uit een Zuidafrikaanse gevangenis* (Baarn: Ten Have, 1988), 70; originally published as *Diary from a South African Prison* (Philadelphia: Fortress Press, 1987).

3. William H. Myers, *God's Yes Was Louder Than My No: Rethinking the African-American Call to Ministry* (Grand Rapids, Mich.: Eerdmans, 1994).

4. Marie-Louise Martin, *Kimbangu: An African Prophet and His Church* (Oxford: Blackwell, 1975), notably 44ff.

5. Gerrie ter Haar, *Halfway to Paradise: African Christians in Europe* (Cardiff: Cardiff Academic Press, 1998).

6. Daniel Himmans-Arday, *And the Truth Shall Set You Free* (London: Janus, 1996).

7. Farisani, *Dagboek uit een Zuidafrikaanse gevangenis*, 66–69.

8. *The Short Oxford English Dictionary on Historical Principles* (Oxford: Oxford University Press, 1973), s.v. "miracle."

9. See Gerrie ter Haar, "A Wondrous God: Miracles in Contemporary Africa," *African Affairs* 102, 408 (2003): 409–28, on which the following sections are based.

10. Recent works include, e.g., Andrew Newberg and Mark R. Waldman, *Why We Believe What We Believe: Uncovering Our Biological Need for Meaning, Spirituality, and Truth* (New York: Free Press, 2006).

11. Yair Zakovitch, *The Concept of the Miracle in the Bible* (Tel Aviv: MOD Books), 1991, whose analysis of biblical miracles is followed here.

12. Ibid., 92.

13. Lindsey Hilsum reporting from Nairobi, "Mary Who 'Met Jesus' Invokes Second Coming in Kenya Slum," *Guardian*, 23 June 1988.

14. Mart Bax, *Medjugorje: Religion, Politics and Violence in Rural Bosnia* (Amsterdam: Free University Press, 1995).

15. Gabriel Maindron, *Des Apparitions à Kibeho: Annonce de Marie au coeur de l'Afrique*, Série Pèlerinages, Sanctuaires, Apparitions (Paris: O.E.I.I., 1984).

16. Italian historian Sergio Luzzatto has claimed that Padre Pio used carbolic acid, or phenol, to cause stigmata. *Miracoli e politica nell' Italia del Novecento* (Turin: Enaudi, 2007).

17. Emma Onuoha, "Born to Bleed," *Guardian Sunday Supplement* (Nigeria), 2 April 1989, B1, B4.

18. Gerrie ter Haar, *Spirit of Africa: The Healing Ministry of Archbishop Milingo of Zambia* London: Hurst; Trenton, N.J.: Africa World Press, 1992).

19. Hugo F. Hinfelaar, *History of the Catholic Church in Zambia 1895–1995* (Lusaka: Book World, 2004), notably 184–90.

20. The term "diaspora" is generally used to refer to those living outside their continent of birth. For a critical discussion, see Gerrie ter Haar, "Chosen People: The Concept of Diaspora in the Modern World," in Steven J. Sutcliffe, ed., *Religion: Empirical Studies: A Collection to Mark the 50th Anniversary of the British Association for the Study of Religions* (Aldershot: Ashgate, 2004), 91–106.

21. Ter Haar, *Halfway to Paradise.*

22. Stephen Ellis and Gerrie ter Haar, "Religion and Politics in Sub-Saharan Africa," *Journal of Modern African Studies* 36, 2 (1998): 175–201.

23. Ter Haar, *Spirit of Africa*, 220–22.

24. Cephas N. Omenyo, *Pentecost Outside Pentecostalism: A Study of the Development of Charismatic Renewal in the Mainline Churches in Ghana* (Zoetermeer: Boekencentrum, 2002).

25. Stephen Ellis and Gerrie ter Haar, *Worlds of Power: Religious Thought and Political Practice in Africa* (London: Hurst; New York: Oxford University Press, 2004), chap. 9.

Chapter 5. The Problem of Evil: Religion and Human Rights in Africa

1. See, e.g., Stephen Ellis, *The Mask of Anarchy: The Destruction of Liberia and the Religious Dimension of an African Civil War* (London: Hurst; New York: New York University Press, 1999).

2. Cf. Joseph Runzo, "Secular Rights and Religious Responsibilities," in Joseph Runzo, Nancy M. Martin, and Arvind Sharma, eds., *Human Rights and Responsibilities in the World Religions*, Library of Global Ethics and Religion 4 (Oxford: Oneworld, 2003), 10; Gerrie ter Haar, *Rats, Cockroaches and People like Us: Views of Humanity and Human Rights*, inaugural address (The Hague: Institute of Social Studies, 2000); see also Runzo et al., 79–95.

3. Ter Haar, "Rats, Cockroaches and People like Us."

4. As Ghanaian philosopher Kwasi Wiredu has argued, for example, with specific reference to the Akan; see Kwasi Wiredu, "An Akan Perspective on Human Rights," in Abdullahi An-Na`im and Francis Deng, eds., *Human Rights in Africa: Cross-Cultural Perspectives* (Washington, D.C.: Brookings Institution Press, 1990), 243–60.

5. Ter Haar, *Rats, Cockroaches and People like Us.*

6. Vikram Dodd, "More Children 'Victims of Cruel Exorcisms,'" *The Guardian*, 4 June 2005, 10.

7. Peter Sarpong, *Ghana in Retrospect: Some Aspects of Ghanaian Culture* (Accra/Tema: Ghana Publishing, 1974), 46–47.

8. Gerrie ter Haar, "Ghanaian Witchcraft Beliefs: A View from the Netherlands," in Gerrie ter Haar, ed., *Imagining Evil: Witchcraft Beliefs and Accusations in Contemporary Africa* (Trenton, N.J.: Africa World Press, 2007), 93–112.

9. Sarpong, *Ghana in Retrospect*, 46.

10 The figure was designed by Walter E. A. van Beek; see "The Escalation of Witchcraft Accusations," in Ter Haar, ed., *Imagining Evil*, 308.

11 Elom Dovlo, "Witchcraft in Contemporary Ghana," in Ter Haar, ed., *Imagining Evil*, 67–92.

12 Comfort Ntiamoah-Mensah, "Gambaga Outcast Home: The Experiences of the Presbyterian Church of Ghana," Paper presented at the International Workshop on Religion and Human Rights, Dodowa, 4–8 November 2002.

Chapter 6. Abundant Life in Africa: Religion and Development

1. Danah Zohar and Ian Marshall, *Spiritual Capital: Wealth We Can Live By* (London: Bloomsbury, 2004), 4.

2. Wendy R. Tyndale, "Towards a Sustainable Development: A Shift in Values," *Commentary* 1, 8 (2001): 3.

3. See Laurenti Magesa, *African Religion: The Moral Traditions of an Abundant Life* (Maryknoll, N.Y.: Orbis, 1997).

4. Bob Goudzwaard, "Religie en ontwikkelingssamenwerking: rem of impuls?" paper presented at a workshop on the role of religion in development processes, The Hague, 8 February 2004.

5. Denis Goulet, "Development Experts: The One-Eyed Giants," *World Development* 8, 7–8 (1980): 481.

6. See Sharon M. P. Harper, ed., *The Lab, the Temple, and the Market: Reflections at the Intersection of Science, Religion, and Development* (Ottawa: International Development Research Centre, 2000).

7. Ibid.; see also relevant World Bank publications such as Katherine Marshall and Lucy Keough, *Mind, Heart, and Soul in the Fight Against Poverty* (Washington, D.C.: World Bank, 2004), and Katherine Marshall and Marisa Van Saanen, *Development and Faith: Where Mind, Heart and Soul Work Together* (Washington, D.C.: World Bank 2007).

8. See Gregory Baum, "Solidarity with the Poor," in Harper, ed., *The Lab, the Temple and the Market*, 72–74.

9. Quoted in ibid., 75.

10. Ibid., 76.

11. United Nations Development Programme, 2006 at http://hdr.undp.org/hd/.

12. Cf. Wendy R. Tyndale, "Poverty and Development: Has Religion a Contribu-

tion to Make?" *Commentary*, 1, 2 (2001): 1–5; also Tyndale, ed., *Visions of Development: Faith-Based Initiatives* (Aldershot: Ashgate, 2006).

13. David Lan, *Guns and Rain: Guerrillas and Spirit Mediums in Zimbabwe* (London: James Currey, 1985).

14. Marthinus L. Daneel, *African Earthkeepers: Wholistic Interfaith Mission* (Maryknoll, N.Y.: Orbis, 2001), on which this account is based.

15. Stephen Ellis and Gerrie ter Haar, *Worlds of Power: Religious Thought and Political Practice in Africa* (London: Hurst; New York: Oxford University Press, 2004), 46; also J. Matthew Schoffeleers, "The AIDS Pandemic, the Prophet Billy Chisupe, and the Democratization Process in Malawi," *Journal of Religion in Africa* 39, 4 (1999): 406–41.

16. Magesa, *African Religion*, chap. 3.

17. See notably Paul Gifford, *Ghana's New Christianity: Pentecostalism in a Globalising African Economy* (London: Hurst, 2004).

18. Andrew F. Walls, "Christian Scholarship and the Demographic Transformation of the Church," in Rodney L. Petersen, ed., with Nancy M. Rourke, *Theological Literacy for the Twenty-First Century* (Grand Rapids, Mich.: Eerdmans, 2002), 177.

19. E. Kingsley Larbi, *Pentecostalism: The Eddies of Ghanaian Christianity* (Accra: Centre for Pentecostal and Charismatic Sudies, 2001), 313.

20. Allan H. Anderson, "Pentecostal Pneumatology and African Power Concepts: Continuity or Change?" *Missionalia* 1 (1991): 72.

21. See the RCCG website at http://www.rccg.org, particularly http://rapac.rccgnet.org/.

22. Emmanuel Milingo, *Development: An African View* (Box Hill, Victoria: Scripture Keys Ministries Australia, 1994), 4; originally mimeograph, 1976.

23. Ibid., 34.

24. Ibid., 4.

25. Ibid.

26. Emmanuel Milingo, *The Mbuliuli Economic Principle*, Phase One, Two, and Three (Zagarolo, 2004–5; privately circulated).

27. Ibid., 22.

28. Ibid., 33.

29. Successive UNDP Reports have stipulated that economic growth is a necessary but not sufficient condition for human development.

30. I have argued this in more detail in connection to questions of conflict and peace. See Gerrie ter Haar, "Religion: Source of Conflict or Resource for Peace?" in Gerrie ter Haar and James J. Busuttil, eds., *Bridge or Barrier: Religion, Violence and Visions for Peace* (Leiden: Brill, 2005), 1–26.

31. Ter Haar, "Religion: Source of Conflict or Resource for Peace?" notably 22–26.

32. Some concrete examples are discussed in Gerrie ter Haar and Stephen Ellis, "The Role of Religion in Development: Towards a New Relationship Between the European Union and Africa," *European Journal of Development Research* 18, 3 (2006): 351–67.

Chapter 7. A Valley of Dry Bones: African Christians Going Global

1. Stephen Ellis and Gerrie ter Haar, *Worlds of Power: Religious Thought and Political Practice in Africa* (London: Hurst; New York: Oxford University Press, 2004), chap. 9.

2. Gerrie ter Haar, "Enchantment and Identity: African Christians in Europe," *Archives de Sciences Sociales des Religions* 143 (July–September 2008), 31–47.

3. Rosalind L. J. Hackett, "Revitalization in African Traditional Religion," in Jacob K. Olupona, ed., *African Traditional Religions in Contemporary Society* (New York: Paragon House, 1991), 135–49.

4. For a full-length study, see Gerrie ter Haar, *Halfway to Paradise: African Christians in Europe* (Cardiff: Cardiff Academic Press, 1998).

4. See RCCG website at http://www.rccg.org.

5. Church of Pentecost, *Know Your Mission Areas: The Church of Pentecost International Missions* (Accra: Pentecost Press, n.d.), 41.

6. Kwabena Asamoah-Gyadu, "African Initiated Christianity in Eastern Europe: Church of the 'Embassy of God' in Ukraine," *International Bulletin of Missionary Research* 30, 2 (2006): 73–75.

7. See Patrick Kalilombe, "Black Christianity in Britain," in Gerrie ter Haar, ed., *Strangers and Sojourners: Religious Communities in the Diaspora* (Leuven: Peeters, 1998), 173–93.

8. Nelly Robin, *Atlas des migrations ouest-africaines vers l'Europe 1985–1993* (Paris: ORSTOM, 1996), 7.

9. John Murray, "Migration and European Society: A View from the Council of Europe," in Han Entzinger and Jack Carter, eds., *Immigration in Western Democracies: The United States and Western Europe*, International Review of Comparative Public Policy 1 (Greenwich, Conn.: JAI Press, 1989), 180.

10. This notably concerns the Spanish enclaves on the North African coast, Ceuta and Melilla, both considered weak spots in the defense of Fortress Europe. In Ceuta the European Union financed a barbed wire fence around the enclave; see Matthew Carr, "Policing the Frontier: Ceuta and Melilla," in Liz Fekete, ed., *Europe: The Wages of Racism*, *Race and Class* 39, 1 (1997): 61–66. Since then, new, higher walls have been erected to try to put a halt to migration from Africa to Europe. Similar solutions to "illegal" immigration can now be observed all over the world.

11. Cf. Ruth Marshall, "'God Is Not a Democrat': Pentecostalism and Democratisation in Nigeria," in Paul Gifford, ed., *The Christian Churches and the Democratisation of Africa* (Leiden: Brill, 1995), 239–60.

12. Walter J. Hollenweger, "Priorities in Pentecostal Research: Historiography, Missiology, Hermeneutics and Pneumatology," in Jan A. B. Jongeneel, ed., *Experiences of the Spirit: Conference on Pentecostal and Charismatic Research in Europe at Utrecht University 1989* (Frankfurt/M.: Peter Lang, 1991), 7–22.

13. Gerrie ter Haar, "Ghanaian Witchcraft Beliefs: A View from the Netherlands," in Ter Haar, ed., *Imagining Evil: Witchcraft Beliefs and Accusations in Contemporary Africa* (Trenton, N.J.: Africa World Press, 2007), 92–112.

14. See http://www.womentrafficking.nl.

Bibliography

An-Naʿim, Abdullahi Ahmed, and Francis M. Deng, eds. *Human Rights in Africa: Cross-Cultural Perspectives*. Washington, D.C.: Brookings Institution Press, 1990.

Anderson, Allan H. *An Introduction to Pentecostalism: Global Charismatic Christianity*. Cambridge: Cambridge University Press, 2004.

———. "Pentecostal Pneumatology and African Power Concepts: Continuity or Change?" *Missionalia* 1 (1991): 65–74.

———. "Types and Butterflies: African Initiated Churches and European Typologies." *International Bulletin of Missionary Research* 25, 3 (2001): 107–13.

Asamoah-Gyadu, Kwabena. "African Initiated Christianity in Eastern Europe: Church of the 'Embassy of God' in Ukraine." *International Bulletin of Missionary Research* 30, 2 (2006): 73–75.

Barrett, David B., and Todd M. Johnson. "Annual Statistical Table on Global Mission: 2004." *International Bulletin of Missionary Research* 28, 1 (2004): 25–26.

———. "Annual Statistical Table on Global Mission: 2008." *International Bulletin of Missionary Research* 32, 1 (2008): 29–30.

Baum, Gregory. "Solidarity with the Poor." In Harper, ed., *The Lab, the Temple, and the Market*, 61–103.

Bax, Mart. *Medjugorje: Religon, Politics and Violence in Rural Bosnia*. Amsterdam: Free University Press, 1995.

Bediako, Kwame. *Christianity in Africa: The Renewal of a Non-Western Religion*. Edinburgh: Edinburgh University Press, 1995.

Behrend, Heike. *Alice Lakwena and the Holy Spirits: War in Northern Uganda, 1986–97*. 1993. Trans. Mick Cohen. Oxford: James Curry, 1999.

Bourguignon, Erika, ed. *Religion, Altered States of Consciousness, and Social Change*. Columbus: Ohio State University Press, 1973.

Brzezinski, Zbigniew. *Out of Control: Global Turmoil on the Eve of the Twenty-First Century*. New York: Scribner, 1993.

Carr, Matthew. "Policing the Frontier: Ceuta and Melilla." In Liz Fekete, ed., *Europe: The Wages of Racism. Race and Class* 39, 1 (1997): 61–66.

Chalmers, David John. *The Conscious Mind: In Search of a Fundamental Theory*. New York: Oxford University Press, 1996.

Church of Pentecost. *Know Your Mission Areas: The Church of Pentecost International Missions*. Accra: Pentecost Press, n.d.

Daneel, Marthinus L. *African Earthkeepers: Wholistic Interfaith Mission*. Maryknoll, N.Y.: Orbis, 2001.

Dovlo, Elom. "Witchcraft in Contemporary Ghana." In Ter Haar, ed., *Imagining Evil.* 67–92.

Ellis, Stephen. *The Mask of Anarchy: The Destruction of Liberia and the Religious Dimension of an African Civil War.* London: Hurst; New York: New York University Press, 1999.

Ellis, Stephen, and Gerrie ter Haar. "Religion and Politics in Sub-Saharan Africa." *Journal of Modern African Studies* 36, 2 (1998): 175–201.

———. *Worlds of Power: Religious Thought and Political Practice in Africa.* London: Hurst; New York: Oxford University Press, 2004.

Elizondo, Virgilio P. *La Morenita: Evangelizer of the Americas.* San Antonio: Mexican American Cultural Center, 1980.

Farisani, Tshenuwani Simon. *Dagboek uit een Zuidafrikaanse Gevangenis.* Baarn: Ten Have, 1988. Originally published as *Diary from a South African Prison.* Philadelphia: Fortress Press, 1987.

Gifford, Paul. *Ghana's New Christianity: Pentecostalism in a Globalising African Economy.* London: Hurst, 2004.

Goodman, Felicitas D. *Ecstasy, Ritual and Alternate Reality: Religion in a Pluralistic World.* Bloomington: Indiana University Press, 1992.

———. *How About Demons? Possession and Exorcism in the Modern World.* Bloomington: Indiana University Press, 1988.

Goudzwaard, Bob. "Religie en ontwikkelingssamenwerking: Rem of impuls?" Paper presented at a workshop on the role of religion in development processes, The Hague, 8 February 2004.

Goulet, Denis. "Development Experts: The One-Eyed Giants." *World Development* 8, 7–8 (1980): 481–89.

Hackett, Rosalind L. J. "Revitalization in African Traditional Religion." In Olupona, ed., *African Traditional Religions.* 135–49.

Harper, Sharon M. P., ed. *The Lab, the Temple, and the Market: Reflections at the Intersection of Science, Religion, and Development.* Ottawa: International Development Research Centre, 2000.

Himmans-Arday, Daniel, *And the Truth Shall Set You Free.* London: Janus, 1996.

Hinfelaar, Hugo F. *Bemba-Speaking Women in a Century of Religious Change (1892–1992).* Leiden: Brill, 1994.

———. *History of the Catholic Church in Zambia 1895–1995.* Lusaka: Book World, 2004.

Hollenweger, Walter J. "Priorities in Pentecostal Research: Historiography, Missiology, Hermeneutics and Pneumatology." In Jan A. B. Jongeneel, ed., *Experiences of the Spirit: Conference on Pentecostal and Charismatic Research in Europe at Utrecht University 1989.* Frankfurt/M.: Peter Lang, 1991. 7–22.

Isichei, Elizabeth. *A History of Christianity in Africa: From Antiquity to the Present.* Grand Rapids, Mich.: Eerdmans; Lawrenceville, N.J.: Africa World Press, 1995.

Jules-Rosette, Bennetta W. "Tradition and Continuity in African Religions: The Case of New Religious Movements." In Olupona, ed., *African Traditional Religions.* 149–65.

Kalilombe, Patrick. "Black Christianity in Britain." In Ter Haar, ed., *Strangers and Sojourners.* 173–93.

Lan, David. *Guns and Rain: Guerrillas and Spirit Mediums in Zimbabwe.* London: James Currey, 1985.

Larbi, E. Kingsley. *Pentecostalism: The Eddies of Ghanaian Christianity.* Accra: Centre for Pentecostal and Charismatic Sudies, 2001.

Luzzatto, Sergio. *Miracoli e politica nell' Italia del Novecento.* Turin: Enaudi, 2007.

Magesa, Laurenti, *African Religion: The Moral Traditions of an Abundant Life.* Maryknoll, N.Y.: Orbis, 1997.

———. *Anatomy of Inculturation: Transforming the Church in Africa.* Maryknoll, N.Y.: Orbis, 2004.

Maindron, Gabriel. *Des Apparitions à Kibeho: Annonce de Marie au coeur de l'Afrique.* Série Pèlerinages, Sanctuaires, Apparitions. Paris: O.E.I.I., 1984.

Malan, Rian. *My Traitor's Heart: A South African Exile Returns to Face His Country, His Tribe, and His Conscience.* London: Bodley Head, 1990.

Marshall, Katherine, and Lucy Keough. *Mind, Heart, and Soul in the Fight Against Poverty.* Washington, D.C.: World Bank, 2004.

Marshall, Katherine, and Marisa Van Saanen, *Development and Faith: Where Mind, Heart and Soul Work Together.* Washington, D.C.: World Bank, 2007.

Marshall, Ruth. "'God Is Not a Democrat': Pentecostalism and Democratisation in Nigeria." In Paul Gifford, ed., *The Christian Churches and the Democratisation of Africa.* Leiden: Brill, 1995. 239–60.

Martin, Marie-Louise. *Kimbangu: An African Prophet and His Church.* Oxford: Blackwell, 1975.

Masuzawa, Tomoko. "Theory Without Method: Situating a Discourse Analysis on Religion." In Ter Haar and Tsuruoka, eds., *Religion and Society.* 173–204.

Meyer, Birgit. "Christianity in Africa: From African Independent to Pentecostal-Charismatic Churches." *Annual Review of Anthropology* 33 (2004): 447–74.

Milingo, Emmanuel. *The Church of the Spirits: Is It to Blame?* Second of a series of pamphlets on the healing ministry. Lusaka, 1978.

———. *The Demarcations.* Lusaka: Teresianum Press, 1982.

———. *Development: An African View.* 1976, mimeograph. Reprinted Broadford, Victoria: Scripture Keys Ministries Australia, 1994.

———. *Healing: "If I Tell You, You Will Not Believe Me!".* Lusaka, 1976/7. First of a series of pamphlets on the healing ministry. Reprinted under the title *Healing with the Power of the Lord Jesus Christ.* Broadford, Victoria: Scripture Keys Ministries Australia, 1994.

———. *Liberation Through Christ: African Point of View.* Lectures given at the Divine Word Centre, London, Ontario, 12–16 April 1977. Mimeographed.

———. *The Mbuliuli Economic Principle.* Phase One, Two, and Three. Zagarolo, 2004–5. Privately circulated.

———. *Plunging into Darkness.* Munich, 1978. Third of a series of pamphlets on the healing ministry. Reprinted Broadford, Victoria: Scripture Keys Ministries Australia, 1993.

———. *Precautions in the Ministry of Deliverance.* Munich, 1978. Fourth of a series of pamphlets on the healing ministry. Reprinted Broadford, Victoria: Scripture Keys Ministries Australia, 1994.

Moore, Sally Falk. *Anthropology and Africa: Changing Perspectives on a Changing Scene*. Charlottesville: University Press of Virginia, 1994.

Murray, John. "Migration and European Society: A View from the Council of Europe." In Han Entzinger and Jack Carter, eds., *Immigration in Western Democracies: The United States and western Europe*. International Review of Comparative Public Policy 1. Greenwich, Conn.: JAI Press, 1989. 179–88.

Myers, William H. *God's Yes Was Louder Than My No: Rethinking the African-American Call to Ministry*. Grand Rapids, Mich.: Eerdmans, 1994.

Nandi, Jack. "The Jerusalem Church of Christ: A Historical and Theological Analysis." MA Thesis, Department of Religion, University of Nairobi, 1993.

Newberg, Andrew, Eugene G. d'Aquili, and Vince Rause. *Why God Won't Go Away: Brain Science and the Biology of Belief*. New York: Ballantine, 2001.

Newberg, Andrew, and Mark R. Waldman. *Why We Believe What We Believe: Uncovering Our Biological Need for Meaning, Spirituality, and Truth*. New York: Free Press, 2006.

Ntiamoah-Mensah, Comfort. "Gambaga Outcast Home: The Experiences of the Presbyterian Church of Ghana." Paper presented at the International Workshop on Religion and Human Rights, Dodowa, 4–8 November, 2002.

Nyamu-Musembi, Celestine, and Andrea Cornwall. "What Is the 'Rights-Based Approach' All About? Perspectives from International Development Agencies." IDS Working Paper 234. Institute of Development Studies, Brighton, Sussex, November 2004.

Okri, Ben. *The Famished Road*. London: Jonathan Cape, 1991.

Olupona, Jacob K., ed. *African Traditional Religions in Contemporary Society*. New York: Paragon House, 1991.

Omenyo, Cephas N. *Pentecost Outside Pentecostalism: A Study of the Development of Charismatic Renewal in the Mainline Churches in Ghana*. Zoetermeer: Boekencentrum, 2002.

Oosthuizen, Gerhardus C. "The African Independent Churches' Centenary." *Africa Insight* 15, 2 (1985): 70–80.

Overholt, Thomas W. *Channels of Prophecy: The Social Dynamics of Prophetic Activity*. Minneapolis: Fortress Press, 1989.

Penrose, Roger. *The Emperor's New Mind: Concerning Computers, Minds, and the Laws of Physics*. Oxford: Oxford University Press, 1989.

———. *Shadows of the Mind: A Search for the Missing Science of Consciousness*. Oxford: Oxford University Press, 1994.

Platvoet, Jan G. "The Religions of Africa in Their Historical Order." In Platvoet, Cox, and Olupona, eds., *The Study of Religions in Africa*. 46–102.

Platvoet, Jan G., James L. Cox, and Jacob K. Olupona, eds. *The Study of Religions in Africa: Past, Present and Prospects*. Cambridge: Roots and Branches, 1996.

Ranger, Terence O. "African Traditional Religion." In Stewart Sutherland and Peter Clarke, eds., *The Study of Religion, Traditional and New Religions*. London: Routledge, 1991. 106–14.

Robin, Nelly. *Atlas des migrations ouest-africaines vers l'Europe 1985–1993*. Paris: ORSTOM, 1996.

Ronca, Italo. "What's in Two Names: Old and New Thoughts on the History and Etymology of *Religio* and *Superstitio*." In Serafino Prete, ed., *Res Publica Literarum: Studies in the Classical Tradition* 15, 1 (1992): 43–60.

Runzo, Joseph. "Secular Rights and Religious Responsibilities." In Runzo, Martin and Sharma, eds., *Human Rights and Responsibilities in the World Religions*. 9–25.

Runzo, Joseph, Nancy M. Martin, and Arvind Sharma, eds. *Human Rights and Responsibilities in the World Religions*. Oxford: Oneworld, 2003

Sarpong, Peter. *Ghana in Retrospect: Some Aspects of Ghanaian Culture*. Accra/Tema: Ghana Publishing, 1974.

Schoffeleers, J. Matthew. "Christ as the Medicine-Man and the Medicine-Man as Christ: A Tentative History of African Christological Thought." *Man and Life* 8, 1, 2 (1982): 11–28.

———. "The AIDS Pandemic, the Prophet Billy Chisupe, and the Democratization Process in Malawi." *Journal of Religion in Africa* 3, 4 (1999): 406–41.

Sheldrake, Rupert. *A New Science of Life: The Hypothesis of Formative Causation*. Los Angeles: Tarcher, 1981.

———. *The Presence of the Past: Morphic Resonance and the Habits of Nature*. New York: Times Books, 1988.

Taylor, Charles, *Multiculturalism: Examining the Politics of Recognition*. Princeton, N.J.: Princeton University Press, 1994.

Ter Haar, Gerrie. "Chosen People: The Concept of Diaspora in the Modern World." In Steven J. Sutcliffe, ed., *Religion: Empirical Studies. A Collection to Mark the 50th Anniversary of the British Association for the Study of Religions*. Aldershot: Ashgate, 2004. 91–106.

———. "Enchantment and Identity: African Christians in Europe." *Archives de Sciences Sociales des Religions* 143 (July–September 2008): 31–47.

———. "Ghanaian Witchcraft Beliefs : A View from the Netherlands." In Ter Haar, ed., *Imagining Evil*. 93–112.

———. *Halfway to Paradise: African Christians in Europe*. Cardiff: Cardiff Academic Press, 1998.

———. ed. *Imagining Evil: Witchcraft Beliefs and Accusations in Contemporary Africa*. Trenton, N.J.: Africa World Press, 2007.

———. *Rats, Cockroaches, and People like Us: Views of Humanity and Human Rights*. The Hague: Institute of Social Studies, 2000. Runzo, Martin, and Sharma, eds., *Human Rights and Responsibilities in the World Religions*. 79–95.

———. "Religion: Source of Conflict or Resource for Peace?" In Gerrie ter Haar and James J. Busuttil, eds., *Bridge or Barrier: Religion, Violence and Visions for Peace*. Leiden: Brill, 2005. 1–26.

———. *Spirit of Africa: The Healing Ministry of Archbishop Milingo of Zambia*. London: Hurst; Trenton, N.J.: Africa World Press, 1992.

———. ed. *Strangers and Sojourners: Religious Communities in the Diaspora*. Leuven: Peeters, 1998

———. "A Wondrous God: Miracles in Contemporary Africa." *African Affairs* 102, 408 (2003): 409–28.

————. *World Religions and Community Religions: Where Does Africa Fit In?* Occasional Paper, Centre of African Studies, University of Copenhagen, 2000.

Ter Haar, Gerrie, and Stephen Ellis. "The Role of Religion in Development: Towards a New Relationship Between the European Union and Africa." *European Journal of Development Research* 18, 3 (2006): 351–67.

Ter Haar, Gerrie, and Yoshio Tsuruoka, eds. *Religion and Society: An Agenda for the 21st Century.* Leiden and Boston: Brill, 2007.

Tillich, Paul. *Theology of Culture.* New York: Oxford University Press, 1959.

Tutuola, Amos. *My Life in the Bush of Ghosts.* London: Faber & Faber, 1954.

Tylor, Edward Burnett. *Primitive Culture.* 1871. Reprinted in two volumes, *The Origins of Culture* and *Religion in Primitive Culture.* New York: Harper, 1958.

Tyndale, Wendy R. "Poverty and Development: Has Religion a Contribution to Make?" *JUST Commentary* 1, 2 (2001): 1–5.

————. "Towards a Sustainable Development: A Shift in Values." *JUST Commentary* 1, 8 (2001): 1–4.

————. ed. *Visions of Development: Faith-Based Initiatives.* Aldershot: Ashgate, 2006.

Van Beek, Walter E. A. "The Escalation of Witchcraft Escalations." In Ter Haar, ed., *Imagining Evil.* 293–315.

Van Lommel, Pim. *Eindeloos Bewustzijn: Een Wetenschappelijke Visie op de Bijna-Dood Ervaring.* Kampen: Ten Have, 2007.

Van Lommel, Pim, Ruud van Wees, Vincent Meyers, and Ingrid Elfferich. "Near-Death Experience in Survivors of Cardiac Arrest: A Prospective Study in the Netherlands." *The Lancet* 358 (2001): 2039–45.

Walls, Andrew F. "Christian Scholarship and the Demographic Transformation of the Church." In Rodney L. Petersen, ed., with Nancy M. Rourke, *Theological Literacy for the Twenty-First Century.* Grand Rapids, Mich.: Eerdmans, 2002. 166–83.

Westerlund, David. *African Religion in African Scholarship: A Preliminary Study of the Religious and Political Background.* Stockholm: Almqvist & Wicksell, 1985.

Wiredu, Kwasi. "An Akan Perspective on Human Rights." In An-Na`im and Deng, eds. *Human Rights in Africa.* 243–60.

Zakovitch, Yair. *The Concept of the Miracle in the Bible.* Tel Aviv: MOD Books, 1991.

Zohar, Danah, and Ian Marshall, *Spiritual Capital: Wealth We Can Live By.* London: Bloomsbury, 2004.

Index

Acknowledgments

As a scholar of religion, I have devoted much of my time to the study of religious developments in Africa, particularly at the interface of Africa's indigenous religions and Christianity. The topics chosen for discussion in this book reflect some of the main themes that I have been working on in my twenty-odd-year academic career, which was preceded by several years of work as an Africa country coordinator for the Dutch section of the international human rights organization Amnesty International. In both capacities I have had the opportunity to learn about the ways many Africans in various parts of the continent involve religion in their daily affairs. The present book is to some extent the outcome of this learning process, as it seeks to combine theoretical insights with the practical experience of people on the ground.

This volume had its impetus in a set of Cunningham Lectures I delivered in November 2006 in the Faculty of Divinity in the University of Edinburgh, under the title "How God Became African: Stories of Religious and Cultural Change." The lecture series is named after William Cunningham (1805–1861), a Scotsman and a strong Calvinist, who was appointed to the Chair of Church History at New College, Edinburgh, of which he became the Principal. New College was founded in 1843, and Edinburgh's Faculty of Divinity is still located there. The Cunningham Lectures series was endowed in 1862 in his memory.

I am grateful to the School of Divinity in the University of Edinburgh for inviting me to deliver the Cunningham Lectures. Special thanks are due to some of the colleagues who facilitated my stay for that purpose, notably Stewart Brown, James Cox, and Jack Thompson.

In the process of writing I have greatly benefited from the support and critical engagement of Stephen Ellis as well as Juliet Pierce, who provided extensive comments on the draft manuscript. I also acknowledge the helpful observations of an anonymous reader, and some useful suggestions made by Bill Finan of the University of Pennsylvania Press to improve on the structure of the book. I am equally grateful to Diel Castelijn, who helped me at the final stage of this book project. To all of them I want to express my heartfelt thanks.